Primary Source and Reading Guide

World History

INTERACTIVE

SAVVAS
LEARNING COMPANY

Cover: Declaration of Independence: Popular and applied graphic art print filing series/Library of Congress Prints and Photographs Division Washington, D.C.[LC-DIG-ppmsca-59409]; Massachusetts Spy 1775 revolutionary newspaper: Old Paper Studios/Alamy Stock Photo; Declaration of the Rights of Man and of the Citizen: PWB Images/Alamy Stock Photo; Post stamp: Ensuper/Shutterstock

Cover Inset: Kneeling Archer, Terracotta Chinese Army: David Davis Photoproductions RF/Alamy Stock Photo; Sarcophagus of Menrekhmut: Martin Thomas Photography/Alamy Stock Photo; American World War II Red Cross Helmet: Chris Howes/Wild Places Photography/Alamy Stock Photo; Leonardo's Horse, Leonardo da Vinci and Nina Akamu: Roman Belogorodov/Alamy Stock Photo; Young Hispanic Woman: David Tiberio/Alamy Stock Photo; Young Indian Man: Michael Jung/Shutterstock; Moctezuma II Headdress: Alexander Klein/AFP/Getty Images; Young Asian Man: Asier Romero/Shutterstock; Young African American Woman: Radius Images/Design Pics/Alamy Stock Photo; British Suffragette: Smith Archive/Alamy Stock Photo; Nelson Mandela: Oistein Thomassen/Alamy Stock Photo; Circuit Board: Raigvi/Shutterstock

ISBN-13: 978-1-418-33040-8
ISBN-10:   1-418-33040-X

2 21

Topic 1 Origins of Civilization (Prehistory–300 B.C.)

Topic 2 The Ancient Middle East and Egypt (3200 B.C.–500 B.C.)

Topic 3 Ancient India and China (3300 B.C.–A.D. 550)

Topic 4 The Americas (Prehistory– A.D. 1570)

Topic 5 Ancient Greece (1750 B.C.–133 B.C.)

Topic 6 Ancient Rome and the Origins of Christianity (509 B.C.– A.D. 476)

Topic 7 Medieval Christian Europe (330–1450)

Topic 8 The Muslim World and Africa (730 B.C.– A.D. 1500)

Topic 9 Civilizations of Asia (500–1650)

Topic 10 The Renaissance and Reformation (1300–1650)

Topic 11 New Global Connections (1415–1796)

Topic 12 Absolutism and Revolution (1550–1850)

Topic 13 The Industrial Revolution (1750–1914)

Topic 14 Nationalism and the Spread of Democracy (1790–1914)

Topic 15 The Age of Imperialism (1800–1914)

Topic 16 World War I and the Russian Revolution (1914–1924)

Topic 17 The World Between the Wars (1910–1939)

Topic 18 World War II (1930–1945)

Topic 19 The Cold War Era (1945–1991)

Topic 20 Developing Nations Emerge (1945–Present)

Topic 21 The World Today (1990–Present)

Lesson 1 Learning About Our Past

CLOSE READING

Studying Prehistory

1. **Summarize** As you read this lesson, fill in an idea web like this one with the kinds of scholars who study the past and what each one does.

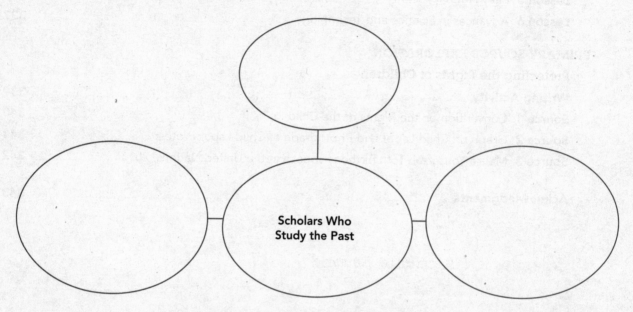

2. **Draw Conclusions** Read "Studying Prehistory." What conclusions can you draw about why historians must consult many sources in order to present a straightforward, unbiased account of events in the past?

3. **Assess an Argument** "Studying Prehistory" compares historians to detectives. Is this an accurate comparison? Explain why you think this comparison is or is not valid.

Investigating Prehistory

4. **Determine Central Ideas** Read "Archaeologists at Work." What main point is made by discussing what we can learn about artifacts from biologists, zoologists, climate scientists, and other kinds of researchers?

5. **Cite Evidence** It can be said that studying prehistory has become a technology-intensive field. Cite evidence from the text that supports this argument.

Discoveries in Africa and Beyond

6. **Cause and Effect** What circumstances led the Leakeys to search for clues to the human past at Olduvai Gorge in East Africa?

7. **Analyze Sequence** Make a list of the hominid groups mentioned in "Discoveries in Africa and Beyond." Assign approximate dates to each group. Use this information to draw conclusions about the development of modern humans.

Lesson 2 The Neolithic Revolution

CLOSE READING

Old Stone Age Skills and Beliefs

1. **Cite Evidence** The text says that early modern humans "found ways to adapt their surroundings to their needs." List examples supporting this statement.

2. **Draw Inferences** Based on your reading, how do archaeologists know what people in the Old Stone Age were eating?

Farming Begins a New Stone Age

3. **Identify Key Steps in a Process** Fill in the key steps to show the transition from the cultures of Paleolithic nomads to those of Neolithic village-dwellers.

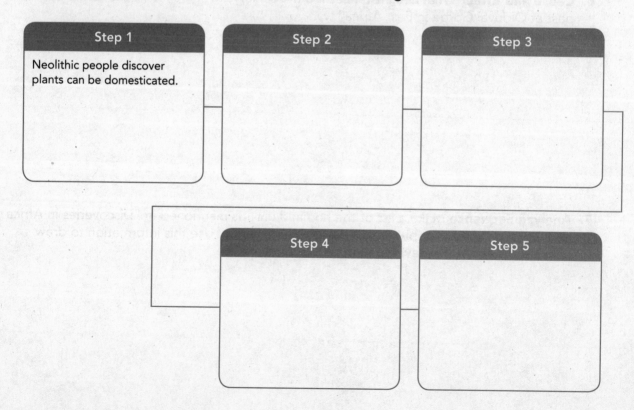

Step 1
Neolithic people discover plants can be domesticated.

Step 2

Step 3

Step 4

Step 5

4. **Draw Inferences** Read the last paragraphs under "The Domestication of Plants and Animals." Draw inferences about why Neolithic people domesticated dogs.

Dramatic Change with the Neolithic Revolution

5. **Identify Supporting Details** About how many years ago were the first large villages built? Explain how you know.

6. **Summarize** In the Neolithic societies, what new groupings of people emerged?

7. **Analyze Interactions** How did a technological innovation (farming) lead to social changes?

Lesson 3 Civilization Begins

CLOSE READING

The First Cities and Civilizations

1. **Analyze Sequence** Beginning with farming, describe the sequence of conditions that brought about the rise of civilizations.

2. **Compare and Contrast** Complete the Venn diagram below to compare and contrast civilizations that began in Asia and Africa with those that begin in the Americas.

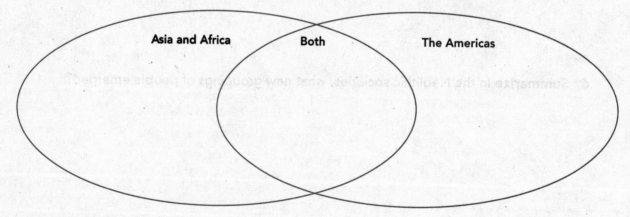

Asia and Africa   Both   The Americas

Features That Define Civilization

3. **Draw Conclusions** Why did cities need complex governments? Cite details from the text to support your answer.

4. **Draw Conclusions** Why was job specialization essential for the development of civilizations?

5. **Identify Cause and Effect** What effects would the invention of writing have on ancient civilizations?

6. **Compare and Contrast** Compare and contrast the civilizations of ancient cities with the nomadic cultures that existed alongside them.

Civilizations Change

7. **Summarize** Summarize the ways in which people living in ancient civilizations depended on the environment.

8. **Paraphrase** Read "Cultural Diffusion." In what ways did cultural diffusion occur?

PRIMARY SOURCE EXPLORATION

The Domestication of Animals

Introduction

The domestication of animals during the Neolithic Age was one of the most important developments in human history. People began to raise animals for many reasons. Some, such as cats and dogs, were pets. But they were often put to work as well. Cats killed rats in grain storehouses, while dogs were used for hunting, herding, and protection. Horses, water buffalo, and camels were other worker species. Many animals became sources of meat — including guinea pigs, raised for food in ancient South America. People also valued animal by-products such as milk, eggs, wool, honey, and silk. Still, there are a lot of unanswered questions about how, when, and where people began to domesticate animals.

Document-Based Writing Activity

Analyze the following four sources and then use information from the documents and your knowledge of world history to write an essay in which you

- Explain the ideas of current scholars about the origins of animal domestication.
- Discuss how people have bred animals for their own use.

Keep in mind that your essay should include an introduction, several paragraphs, and a conclusion. In the body of the essay, use evidence from at least three documents. Support your response with relevant facts, examples, and details. In developing your essay, be sure to keep these general definitions in mind:

- *Explain* means "to make plain or understandable; to give reasons for or causes of; to show the logical development or relationships of."
- *Discuss* means "to make observations about something using facts, reasoning, and argument; to present in some detail."

Source 1

Table of domestication of selected animals

Modern anthropologists and historians do not agree on exactly when various animal species were domesticated. There is general agreement, however, that dogs were domesticated first, and that sheep were among the earliest animals raised for food. This table represents one accepted timeline.

Animal	Approximate Date
dog	Before 10,000 B.C.
sheep, cat	8500 B.C.
goat	8000 B.C.
pig, cattle	7000 B.C.
chicken	6000 B.C.
zebu, guinea pig	5000 B.C.
llama, alpaca	4500 B.C.
donkey	4000 B.C.
horse, silkworm, Bactrian camel	3500 B.C.
honey bee, dromedary, yak	3000 B.C.
water buffalo, duck	2500 B.C.
goose	1500 B.C.
reindeer	1000 B.C.
turkey	100 B.C.–A.D. 100

1. What was the first non-mammal domesticated by people?

2. Pack animals are animals trained to carry loads. Which of the animals on this list were domesticated as pack animals?

3. Which animals could be used as a source of clothing?

Source 2

"When and How Did Wolves Become Dogs?" Brian Handwerk, Smithsonian, *2018*

It is universally agreed that the dog was the first animal domesticated by people. Here, a modern journalist discusses two theories about how that happened.

Long ago, before your four-legged best friend learned to fetch tennis balls or watch football from the couch, his ancestors were purely wild animals in competition—sometimes violent—with our own.... Pugs and poodles may not look the part, but if you trace their lineages far enough back in time all dogs are descended from wolves. . . .

One [theory] argues that early humans somehow captured wolf pups, kept them as pets, and gradually domesticated them. This could have happened around the same time as the rise of agriculture, about 10,000 years ago. The oldest fossils generally agreed to be domestic dogs date to about 14,000 years, but several disputed fossils more than twice that age may also be dogs or at least their no longer entirely wolf ancestors.

Since more recent genetic studies suggest that the date of domestication occurred far earlier, a different theory has gained the support of many scientists. "Survival of the friendliest" suggests that wolves largely domesticated themselves among hunter-gatherer people.

"That the first domesticated animal was a large carnivore, who would have been a competitor for food—anyone who has spent time with wild wolves would see how unlikely it was that we somehow tamed them in a way that led to domestication," says Brian Hare, director of the Duke University Canine Cognition Center.

But, Hare notes, the physical changes that appeared in dogs over time, including splotchy coats, curly tails, and floppy ears, follow a pattern of a process known as self-domestication. It's what happens when the friendliest animals of a species somehow gain an advantage. Friendliness somehow drives these physical changes, which can begin to appear as visible byproducts of this selection in only a few generations. . . .

Hare adds that most wolves would have been fearful and aggressive towards humans—because that's the way most wolves behave. But some would have been friendlier, which may have given them access to human hunter-gatherer foodstuffs. . . . "This is self-domestication. We did not domesticate dogs. Dogs domesticated themselves."

1. How does the author contrast domesticated dogs and their ancestors?

2. Identify two ways the author cites modern science as evidence.

3. Restate in your own words the theory of "survival of the friendliest."

Source 3

Images of Wild and Domesticated Animals

After domesticating animals, prehistoric people learned to breed them selectively. As a result, the animals that developed were the ones most useful to humans.

A wild pig is contrasted with a domesticated pig.

The mouflon—a wild sheep of South Asia—is thought to be the ancestor of all modern domesticated sheep.

1. What differences can you see between the wild and domesticated versions of these animals?

2. Why do you think people bred these animals to develop these traits?

3. Give another example of how people may have bred an animal to develop certain traits.

Source 4

Reasons Why Few Large Wild Animals Were Domesticated

In all of human history, very few species have been successfully domesticated by humans. In his book *Guns, Germs, and Steel*, anthropologist Jared Diamond explained why people were unable to domesticate so many large animals. This chart shows some of the reasons.

Why did early people not domesticate more large animals?		
Reason	**Examples**	**Explanation**
The animal consumes too much food for the benefit it gives to people.	Lions, most carnivores	Since carnivores eat other animals, finding enough food to raise carnivores is too costly.
The animal does not gain maturity quickly enough.	Elephants, gorillas	These animals can take ten years or more to mature, as opposed to other animals that mature in one or two years.
The animal is too fierce to live near humans.	Grizzly bear, hippopotamus	These animals would kill those who tried to tame them.
The animal panics too easily.	Gazelles	These animals would harm themselves and other animals by panicking in a herd or enclosed space.
The animals do not have a social structure that lends itself to domestication.	Cats, African antelopes	These animals are used to living alone, or, if they live in herds, they will not share their territory with rival herds.

Information from *Guns, Germs, and Steel: The Fate of Human Societies*, Jared Diamond, 1999

1. Drawing on this information, what traits do animals need in order for people to be able to domesticate them?

2. Based on this information, why do you think rhinoceroses have not been domesticated?

3. Drawing on this information, infer the role dominance plays in domestication.

Lesson 1 A Civilization Emerges in Sumer

CLOSE READING

Civilizations Arise in the Fertile Crescent

1. **Identify Cause and Effect** What prompted people to work together in early Sumer?

2. **Infer** What might one learn by reading *The Epic of Gilgamesh*?

3. **Integrate Information from Diverse Sources** Read "Sumerian City-States." Then look at the photograph showing buildings from Ur. What do the text and the image convey about Sumerian cities? Is the information in the picture and text consistent? How does the photograph build on your understanding from the text?

Sumerian Civilization Develops

4. **Analyze Interactions** Discuss the relationship between the king and the Sumerian people. What was the role of the king in society?

5. **Identify Important Details** As you read "Social Classes," examine the text for information about the structure of Sumerian society. Then use the graphic organizer below to record the types of people in each social class.

Upper Class	Middle Class	Lower Class

6. **Cite Evidence** How did cuneiform come about? Cite evidence from the text to support your answer.

Sumer's Legacy

7. **Explain** How did the Sumerian civilization influence later civilizations?

8. **Identify Central Ideas** How did Sumerian mathematical and technological ideas spread to other civilizations?

Lesson 2 Empires in Mesopotamia

CLOSE READING

Empires Emerge in Mesopotamia

1. **Identify Important Details** As you read the lesson, examine the text for information about the order of Mesopotamian empires. Then use the timeline below to record names and dates.

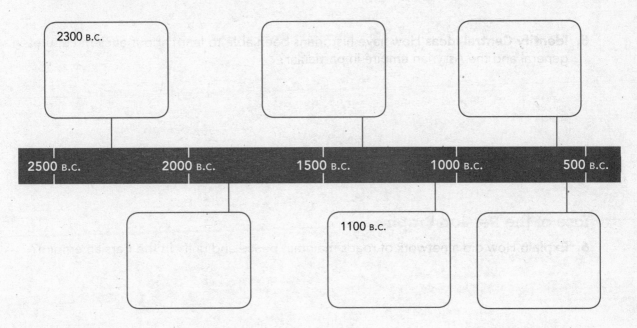

2. **Explain** Why was Hammurabi's Code a great achievement?

3. **Infer** Under Hammurabi's Code, what might happen if a person accidentally did something that caused another person to die?

New Empires and Ideas

4. **Analyze Interactions** Why did the Hittites want to keep their knowledge of how to extract iron from ore secret?

5. **Identify Central Ideas** How have historians been able to learn about ancient cultures in general and the Assyrian empire in particular?

Rise of the Persian Empire

6. **Explain** How did a network of roads maintain peace and unity in the Persian empire?

7. **Contrast** What is the difference between a barter economy and a money economy?

Phoenician Contributions

8. **Identify Cause and Effect** How did Phoenician colonies help spread their civilization?

Lesson 3 The Hebrews and the Origins of Judaism

CLOSE READING

The Ancient Israelites' Unique Belief System

1. **Compare and Contrast** How were the ancient Israelites similar to other Canaanites and how were they different?

The Ancient Israelites

2. **Summarize** Why is Abraham an important figure in Judaism?

3. **Identify Cause and Effect** According to the Book of Genesis, for what reasons did an Egyptian pharaoh enslave the Israelites? How were they freed from their bondage?

4. **Identify Cause and Effect** What happened when Nebuchadnezzar and the Babylonian armies captured Judah?

Judaism's Legacy

5. Identify Central Ideas How did the Ten Commandments shape Judaism?

6. Infer What did the prophets think about the role of wealthy and powerful people in a society?

7. Explain How did the Diaspora contribute to Jewish values spreading to western cultures?

8. Cite Evidence Which concepts of democracy can be traced to Judeo-Christian influences? Cite evidence from the text to support your answer.

Lesson 4 Egyptian Civilization

CLOSE READING

Geography Shapes Egypt

1. **Explain** Why was the flooding of the Nile a benefit for ancient Egyptians? Why was controlling its flooding important?

The Old Kingdom

2. **Identify Cause and Effect** What enabled pharaohs to create a strong, centralized state in ancient Egypt?

Middle and New Kingdom Egypt

3. **Summarize** What were the main accomplishments of the rulers during the New Kingdom?

Religion Shapes Ancient Egyptian Life

4. **Explain** Why was Osiris an important Egyptian god?

5. **Identify Central Ideas** Why were bodies mummified?

Organization of Egyptian Society

6. **Cite Evidence** In what ways did Egyptian women enjoy a higher status than women elsewhere in the ancient world? Cite textual evidence to support your answer.

Egyptian Learning Advances

7. **Identify Cause and Effect** How did the Rosetta Stone enable historians to learn more about ancient Egypt?

8. **Identify Important Details** As you read "Egyptian Learning Advances," examine the text for advances in science and mathematics, arts, and literature. Then use the chart below to record advances.

Science and Mathematics	Arts	Literature

PRIMARY SOURCE EXPLORATION

Harmony, Balance, and the Afterlife in Ancient Egypt

Introduction

In ancient Egypt, an important concept was maat, or social harmony and cosmic balance. To Egyptians, maat allowed the world to function as it should according to the will of the gods. It was the role of the ruler, or pharaoh, to maintain this balance and to model moral behavior. The Egyptian belief in the afterlife also placed great importance on moral behavior. Ancient Egyptians believed that the gods Osiris and Isis had promised them eternal life; to enter the afterlife, the deceased had to pass a test to prove his or her worthiness.

Document-Based Writing Activity

Analyze the following four sources and then use information from the documents and your knowledge of world history to write an essay in which you

- Discuss the importance of moral behavior and the afterlife to ancient Egyptians.

Keep in mind that your essay should include an introduction, several paragraphs, and a conclusion. In the body of the essay, use evidence from at least three documents. Support your response with relevant facts, examples, and details. In developing your essay, be sure to keep this general definition in mind:

- *Discuss* means "to make observations about something using facts, reasoning, and argument; to present in some detail."

Source 1

Instructions of the Vizier Ptah-hotep, c. 2450 B.C.

Ptah-hotep was the vizier, or chief minister, during the reign of Pharaoh Djedkare Isesi around 2450 B.C. He wrote about the virtues necessary to live a good life and maintain social order and harmony in Egypt, such as obedience and humility. His writings were intended primarily for an audience of young men who would one day assume high offices in Egyptian government.

If you have, as leader, to decide on the conduct of a great number of men, seek the most perfect manner of doing so that your own conduct may be without reproach. Justice is great, invariable, and assured... To throw obstacles in the way of the laws is to open the way before violence...

If you are a leader, setting forward your plans according to that which you decide, perform perfect actions which posterity may remember, without letting the words prevail with you which multiply flattery, which excite pride and produce vanity....

If you desire that your conduct should be good and preserved from all evil, keep yourself from every attack of bad humor. It is a fatal malady which leads to discord, and there is no longer any existence for him who gives way to it. For it introduces discord between fathers and mothers, as well as between brothers and sisters; it causes the wife and the husband to hate each other; it contains all kinds of wickedness, it embodies all kinds of wrong. . . .

If you are powerful, respect knowledge and calmness of language. Command only to direct; to be absolute is to run into evil. Let not your heart be haughty, neither let it be mean. Do not let your orders remain unsaid and cause your answers to penetrate; but speak without heat, assume a serious countenance. . . .

Teach others to render homage to a great man. . . .

If you have become great after having been little, if you have become rich after having been poor, when you are at the head of the city, know how not to take advantage of the fact that you have reached the first rank, harden not your heart because of your elevation.... Put not behind you the neighbor who is like you; be unto him as a companion. . . .

If you hear those things which I have said to you, your wisdom will be fully advanced. Although they are the means which are suitable for arriving at the maat, and it is that which makes them precious, their memory would recede from the mouth of men. But thanks to the beauty of their arrangement in rhythm all their words will now be carried without alteration over this earth eternally.

---

1. According to Ptah-hotep, why is justice important?

2. What does "bad humor" lead to, according to this source?

3. In your own words, what is Ptah-hotep saying in the last paragraph?

Source 2

The Weighing of the Heart, c. 1250 B.C.

During the New Kingdom, Egyptians were often buried with copies of the Book of the Dead, an illustrated series of spells and declarations meant to ease the dangerous path through the underworld and into the afterlife. This scene shows the god Anubis (kneeling, with the head of a jackal) weighing the heart of the deceased person against a feather representing Maat, the goddess of truth and balance. If the heart was equal to or lighter than the feather, it was judged to be pure and the virtuous deceased person passed into the afterlife. If not, the unworthy heart was eaten by the creature Ammit (at far right), part crocodile, part lion, and part hippopotamus.

1. What does the central part of this image show?

2. How does the ritual of the weighing of the heart demonstrate Egyptians' beliefs about moral behavior?

3. Why do you think Ammit's body was shown as part crocodile, part lion, and part hippopotamus?

Source 3

The Papyrus of Ani, c. 1250 B.C.

One of the most richly illustrated surviving copies of the Book of the Dead is known as the *Papyrus of Ani*, written around 1250 B.C. for a scribe named Ani. (The image in Source 2 of this activity is taken from the *Papyrus.*) In this passage, Ani's heart has been weighed and found worthy of the afterlife, and the god Horus presents him to Osiris, the god of the dead. (In this passage, Ani is often referred to as *Osiris*, showing the belief that the deceased acquire divine characteristics themselves.)

THE PRAYER OF ANI: May nought stand up to oppose me at [my] judgment, may there be no opposition to me ... and may no lies be spoken against me…

THE SPEECH OF THOTH: Thoth, the judge of right and truth of the Great Company of the Gods who are in the presence of Osiris, saith: Hear ye this judgment. The heart of Osiris hath in very truth been weighed, and his Heart-soul hath borne testimony on his behalf; his heart hath been found right by the trial in the Great Balance. There hath not been found any wickedness in him; he hath not wasted the offerings which have been made in the temples; he hath not committed any evil act; and he hath not set his mouth in motion with words of evil whilst he was upon earth.

THE SPEECH OF THE GODS: ... The Osiris the scribe Ani, whose word is true, is holy and righteous. He hath not committed any sin, and he hath done no evil against us. The devourer Am-mit shall not be permitted to prevail over him.....

THE SPEECH OF HORUS TO OSIRIS IN INTRODUCING ANI TO HIM: ... I have brought unto thee the Osiris Ani. His heart is righteous, and it hath come forth from the Balance; it hath not sinned against any god or any goddess. Thoth hath weighed it according to the decree pronounced unto him by the Company of the Gods, and it is most true and righteous. Grant thou that cakes and ale may be given unto him, and let him appear in the presence of the god Osiris, and let him be like unto the Followers of Horus for ever and ever.

THE SPEECH OF ANI: And the Osiris Ani saith: Behold, I am in thy presence, O Lord of Amentet. There is no sin in my body. I have not spoken that which is not true knowingly, nor have I done anything with a false heart. Grant thou that I may be like unto those favoured ones who are in thy following, and that I may be an Osiris greatly favoured of the beautiful god, and beloved of the Lord of the Two Lands…

1. What is Ani's prayer?

2. Why do you think Ani commissioned the creation of this copy of the Book of the Dead?

3. According to this source, what happened when Ani was judged?

Source 4

The Tomb of Tutankhamen, Howard Carter and A.C. Mace, 1923

In 1922, British archaeologist Howard Carter discovered the long-hidden tomb of the Pharaoh Tutankhamen. He later wrote the following description of what he found. Note that canopic chests are containers used by ancient Egyptians to contain the internal organs removed during the mummification process.

With trembling hands I made a tiny breach in the upper left hand corner....[W]idening the hole a little, I inserted the candle and peered in....[P]resently, as my eyes grew accustomed to the light, details of the room within emerged slowly from the mist, strange animals, statues, and gold—everywhere the glint of gold....

Surely never before in the whole history of excavation had such an amazing sight been seen as the light of our torch revealed to us.... [C]ertainly we had never dreamed of anything like this, a roomful—a whole museumful it seemed—of objects, some familiar, but some the like of which we had never seen, piled one upon another in seemingly endless profusion....

It was, beyond any question, the sepulchral chamber in which we stood, for there, towering above us, was one of the great gilt shrines in which kings were laid.... From top to bottom it was overlaid with gold, and upon its sides there were inlaid panels of brilliant blue faience, in which were represented, repeated over and over, the magic symbols that would ensure its strength and safety. Around the shrine, resting on the ground, there were a number of funerary emblems, and, at the north end, the seven magic oars the king would need to ferry himself across the waters of the underworld....

Facing the doorway, on the farther side, stood the most beautiful monument that I have ever seen—so lovely that it made one gasp with wonder and admiration. The central portion of it consisted of a large shrine-shaped chest, completely overlaid with gold, and surmounted by a cornice of sacred cobras. Surrounding this, freestanding, were statues of the four tutelary goddesses of the dead.... One guarded the shrine on each of its four sides, ... [with two of them] looking over their shoulders towards the entrance, as though to watch against surprise....It is undoubtedly the Canopic chest and contains the jars which play such an important part of the ritual of mummification.

---

1. What do the contents of Tutankhamen's tomb suggest about ancient Egyptians' view of the afterlife?

2. How does the tomb show the importance of its occupant?

3. What does the placement of the canopic chest tell you about its significance?

Lesson 1 Early Civilization in South Asia

CLOSE READING

Geography of the Indian Subcontinent

1. **Integrate Information From Diverse Sources** Read the first three paragraphs of "Geography of the Indian Subcontinent." Then look at the map of India. How does the visual material enhance the text? What does the text tell you that you wouldn't see just by looking at the map? What does the map show you that you didn't read in the text?

2. **Summarize** How do the monsoons affect life in India?

The Forgotten Indus Civilization

3. **Determine Meaning of Words** Reread the section titled "Indus Religious Beliefs." Based on evidence from the text, what does the word *polytheistic* mean? Cite evidence from the text to support your answer.

4. **Summarize** What factors do archaeologists believe led to the decline of the Indus civilization? Why is the decline of the Indus civilization still a mystery?

Vedic Civilization

5. **Compare and Contrast** Compare and contrast the early Indus civilization with the Vedic civilization. Fill out a chart like the one below to help organize your information.

Indus Civilization	Vedic Civilization

6. **Draw Inferences** What factors do you think led to the transition of the Vedic people from nomadic herders to farmers? Cite evidence to support your answer.

The Great Vedic Epics

7. **Compare and Contrast** Reread the text describing both the *Mahabharata* and the *Ramayana*. In what ways do the two texts differ? In what ways are they similar?

Lesson 2 The Origins of Hinduism and Buddhism

CLOSE READING

Hindu Beliefs Develop

1. **Identify Supporting Details** Which details under the heading "One Force Unites Everything" help you understand the quote: "God is one, but wise people know it by many names"? How does this quote give you a better understanding of the basic principles of Hinduism?

2. **Summarize** What are some of the most important principles in Hinduism? Fill in the chart below with information explaining each of these principles.

Principles of Hinduism	
Principle	**Explanation**
Example: atman	the essential self

India's Caste System

3. **Draw Inferences** The text states that "Over time, thousands of birth-based jati developed in India, each with its own religious practices and social customs." How do you think this evolution occurred?

The Buddha's Key Teachings

4. **Analyze Relationships** In Buddhism, what is the relationship between the Four Noble Truths and the Eightfold Path? How do the two concepts explain the most important principles of Buddhism?

5. **Compare and Contrast** Compare and contrast the basic principles of Buddhism with the basic principles of Hinduism. How are the two religions similar, and how do they differ?

Buddhism Spreads

6. **Analyze** What is the importance of the *Tripitaka* to the Buddhist religion? How did the development of the texts support the evolution of Buddhism?

7. **Compare and Contrast** Compare and contrast the two major sects of Buddhism that developed after the death of the Buddha. What factors do you think led to the growth of the Mahayana sect?

Lesson 3 Powerful Empires Emerge in India

CLOSE READING

The Maurya Empire Builds a Strong Government

1. **Analyze** Reread the quote from Ashoka: "I have had banyan trees planted on the roads to give shade to people and animals. I have planted mango groves, and I have had [wells] dug and shelters erected along the roads." What does this quote say about Ashoka's reign in India?

Deccan Kingdoms Arise

2. **Summarize** Read the paragraphs under "Deccan Kingdoms Arise." What were some of the achievements of the Tamil kingdom?

A Golden Age Under Gupta Rulers

3. **Analyze** Read the quotation from Faxian, under "A Time of Peace and Prosperity." "The people are numerous and happy; . . . only those who cultivate the Royal land have to pay [a portion of] the grain from it. . . . The king governs without . . . corporal punishments. Criminals are simply fined, lightly or heavily, according to the circumstances [of each case]." How does this contribute to your understanding of how India functioned under Gupta rule? What does it tell you about the Guptas, as rulers?

4. **Compare and Contrast** Compare and contrast the reigns of the Mauryan emperors and the Guptas. Use the chart below to help organize your information.

The Mauryan Emperors	The Guptas

Family and Village Life Shape Indian Society

5. **Determine Meaning of Words** Read the section "Joint Family Structure." What do you think the word *patriarchal* means? Why do you think it is important to note that Indian families were generally patriarchal? Use evidence from the text to support your answer.

6. **Summarize** How did the role of women in India change from the Vedic period?

7. **Analyze** How did agriculture and trade help shape life in Indian villages? Cite evidence from the text to support your answer.

Lesson 4 Ancient Civilization in China

CLOSE READING

Geography Influences Chinese Civilization

1. **Use Visual Information** Read the paragraphs under "Geography Influences Chinese Civilization." How did geography contribute to the belief that China was the sole source of civilization?

The Shang Dynasty Begins to Form China

2. **Determine Meaning of Words** Read the first paragraph under "The Shang Dynasty Begins to Form China." What do you think the word *dynasty* means? Why would the evolution of dynasties play such an important role in Chinese history?

The Zhou Dynasty

3. **Integrate Information From Diverse Sources** Read the first two paragraphs of "The Zhou Claim the Mandate of Heaven." Then look at the visual explaining the dynastic cycle. What do the text and the image convey about the Zhou dynasty and the Mandate of Heaven? How do these sources work together to increase your understanding of the information?

4. **Draw Inferences** Read the paragraphs under "A Feudal State is Established." Why did the Zhou king grant control of territories to his supporters? How did this make him an effective leader?

Religious Beliefs in Early China

5. **Analyze** Read the section "Veneration of Ancestors." In describing the relationship of the Chinese with the spirits of their ancestors, the text states, "When westerners reached China, they mistakenly called this practice 'ancestor worship.'" Based on your reading, why was the label *ancestor worship* a mistake?

Two Major Belief Systems Take Root

6. **Integrate Information From Diverse Sources** Read the quotes from the *Analects* that accompany the text about Confucius. How do these quotes further your understanding of the teachings of Confucius? What do they tell you about Confucian philosophy?

7. **Compare and Contrast** Compare and contrast the philosophies of Confucianism and Daoism. Note the similarities and differences in history and ideology. Use the Venn Diagram below to organize your information.

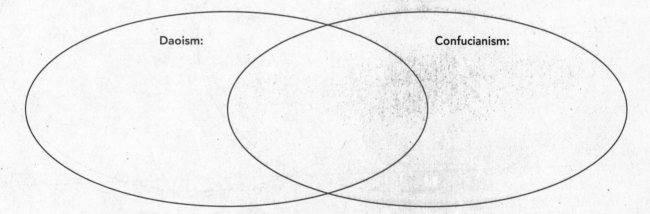

Daoism:

Confucianism:

A Time of Achievements in Early China

8. **Identify Supporting Details** Read the section "The Time of Achievements in Early China." Which details from the text support this heading?

Lesson 5 Strong Rulers Unite China

CLOSE READING

Shi Huangdi Unifies China

1. **Identify Supporting Details** Read the section "Emperor Centralizes Power." How did Shi Huangdi force unity in China? Which details from the text support this idea?

The Han Dynasty Creates a Strong China

2. **Compare and Contrast** Compare and contrast the reign of Wudi with the reign of Shi Huangdi. Which ruling principles and historical advancements were specific to each leader, and which did they have in common? Use the chart below to organize your information.

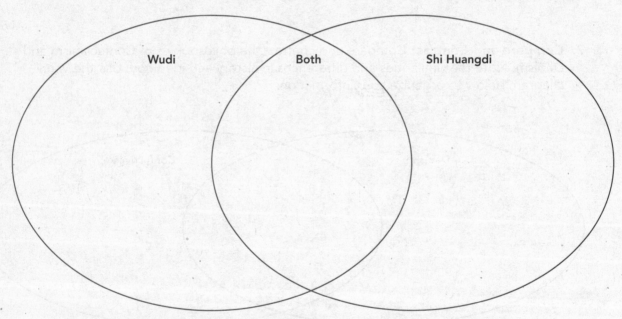

Wudi   Both   Shi Huangdi

3. **Synthesize Information** Describe the Silk Road. How was the Silk Road an important part of the growth of civilization in China?

The Han Golden Age

4. **Cite Evidence** Why was the era of Han rule considered a Golden Age in China? Cite evidence from the text to support your answer.

5. **Summarize** What was the role of women during the Han Golden Age in China?

Buddhism Spreads to China

6. **Summarize** Why was the spread of Buddhism in China initially met with resistance?

7. **Determine Meaning of Words** Read the third paragraph of "Buddhism Spreads to China." Recall what the phrase *filial piety* means. How does the concept of filial piety relate to Buddhist principles?

PRIMARY SOURCE EXPLORATION

Governing China: A Legacy of Strong Central Control

Introduction

The ancient Chinese empire spread over an enormous region. Shi Huangdi, or First Emperor, united China in 221 B.C. Adhering to a philosophy of legalism, he molded the kingdom to his will. He set up a system of government that forced diverse peoples to follow standardized systems of laws, weights and measures, writing, and currency. He also enacted many reforms, encouraged cultural and intellectual advancement, and created huge construction projects, such as the Great Wall. But his control was brutal, allowing for no dissent. As different dynasties arose over succeeding centuries, his style of both harsh rule and national advancement were a model for many of China's leaders. The communist government of China may be the latest successor to his model of leadership. Under Mao Zedong, the nation was once again molded to the desires and thoughts of one strong leader.

Document-Based Writing Activity

Analyze the following four sources, and then use information from the documents and your knowledge of world history to write an essay in which you

- Compare how the governments of Shi Huangdi and Mao Zedong ruled China's people.
- Discuss the long-term results of their rule on China.

Keep in mind that your essay should include an introduction, several paragraphs, and a conclusion. In the body of the essay, use evidence from at least three documents. Support your response with relevant facts, examples, and details. In developing your essay, be sure to keep these general definitions in mind.

- *Compare* means "to find similarities between two ideas or documents."
- *Discuss* means "to make observations about something using facts, reasoning, and argument; to present in some detail."

Source 1

Terracotta Army of Shi Huangdi, c. 210 B.C.

Obsessed with his own mortality and fearful of conquered enemies in the afterlife, Shi Huangdi had an army built of terracotta to protect him in an elaborate tomb complex, shown here. The terracotta figures included soldiers, horses, chariots, as well as government officials, musicians, and acrobats. There were also real tools, weapons, and animal sculptures made of bronze.

1. What does this image of the tomb tell you about Shi Huangdi's rule?

2. What can you infer about civilization at the time?

3. How does this help us understand the spiritual beliefs and values of Shi Huangdi?

Source 2

"Memorial on the Burning of the Books," Attributed to Li Si by Sima Qian (c. 90 B.C.), in *Sources of Chinese Tradition: From Earliest Times to 1600,* Compiled by William Theodore de Bary, Irene Bloom, and Joseph Adler, 1999

Li Si served as adviser to Shi Huangdi. Following his advice, Shi Huangdi unified the warring Chinese states and improved the economic and cultural life of the peoples. Embracing the philosophy of legalism, Li Si advocated efficient and ruthless control. He suppressed criticism and individual thought by destroying critical books, scholars, and officials.

In earlier times the empire disintegrated and fell into disorder, and no one was capable of unifying it. Thereupon the various feudal lords rose to power. In their discourses they all praised the past in order to disparage the present and embellished empty words to confuse the truth. . . . But at present Your Majesty possesses a unified empire . . . and has firmly established for yourself a position of sole supremacy. And yet these independent schools, joining with each other, criticize the codes of laws and instructions. Hearing of the promulgation of a decree, they criticize it, each from the standpoint of his own school. At home they disapprove of it in their hearts; going out they criticize it in the [street]. They seek a reputation by discrediting their sovereign; they appear superior by expressing contrary views, and they lead the lowly multitude in the spreading of slander. If such license is not prohibited, the sovereign power will decline above and partisan factions will form below. It would be well to prohibit this.

Your servant suggests that all books in the imperial archives, save the memoirs of Qin, be burned. All persons in the empire, except members of the Academy of Learned Scholars, in possession of the Classic of Odes, the Classic of Documents, and discourses of the hundred philosophers should take them to the local governors and have them indiscriminately burned.

Those who dare to talk to each other about the Odes and Documents should be executed and their bodies exposed in the marketplace. Anyone referring to the past to criticize the present should, together with all members of his family, be put to death. Officials who fail to report cases that have come under their attention are equally guilty. After thirty days from the time of issuing the decree, those who have not destroyed their books are to be branded and sent to build the Great Wall. Books not to be destroyed will be those on medicine and pharmacy, [prophecy], and agriculture and arboriculture.

1. Why did Li Si want to suppress independent thought?

2. How did Li Si distinguish between which books to ban and which to allow?

3. What were the consequences for criticizing these rules?

Source 3

"On the Correct Handling of Contradictions Among the People," Speech by Mao Zedong, February 27, 1957

Mao Zedong led the Chinese Communist Party. Under Mao, the communists put all industry and agriculture under state control. Mao would not tolerate any challenges to his leadership or communist control.

The Question of the Intellectuals

. . . It seems as if Marxism, once all the rage, is currently not so much in fashion. To counter these tendencies, we must strengthen our ideological and political work. Both students and intellectuals should study hard. In addition to the study of their specialized subjects, they must make progress ideologically and politically, which means they should study Marxism, current events and politics. Not to have a correct political orientation is like not having a soul.

On "Let a Hundred Flowers Blossom Let a Hundred Schools of Thought Contend" and "Long-Term Coexistence and Mutual Supervision"

. . . In their political activities, how should our people judge whether a person's words and deeds are right or wrong? On the basis of the principles of our Constitution, the will of the overwhelming majority of our people and the common political positions which have been proclaimed on various occasions by our political parties, we consider that, broadly speaking, the criteria should be as follows:

(1) Words and deeds should help to unite, and not divide, the people of all our nationalities.
(2) They should be beneficial, and not harmful, to socialist transformation and socialist construction.
(3) They should help to consolidate, and not undermine or weaken, the people's democratic dictatorship.
(4) They should help to consolidate, and not undermine or weaken, democratic centralism.
(5) They should help to strengthen, and not shake off or weaken, the leadership of the Communist Party.
(6) They should be beneficial, and not harmful, to international socialist unity and the unity of the peace-loving people of the world. . . .

---

1. What does the sentence "Marxism … is currently not so much in fashion?" mean?

2. How did Mao want to counter the trend of Marxism not being in favor?

3. Does the heading above the second paragraph represent the six criteria that are listed? Why or why not?

Source 4

"Eyewitness of the Cultural Revolution," by a "Foreign Expert," China Quarterly, 1966

In 1966, Mao Zedong launched the Cultural Revolution to consolidate his power. The government closed schools, forced farmers into state communes, and organized Chinese youth as "Red Guards." The Red Guards punished anyone seen as not "revolutionary" enough. The result was chaos and destruction. The author of this eyewitness account withheld his name to protect his sources.

Violence, torture and humiliation seem to have been less marked – or better concealed– in [Beijing] than elsewhere, though we saw enough. In [Tianjin], for instance, people were seen being made to kneel, either in the street or on narrow raised planks for several hours at a stretch, heads bent and arms raised. They were constantly reviled, prodded and beaten, made to confess their crimes, then paraded round the town in groups. When asked how they chose their victims, one Red Guard said that a group would think hard about the people they knew until someone remembered, for instance, that in the past a certain woman had worn cosmetics or frequently had her hair permed. The group would then proceed to the woman's home and point out the error of her ways. . . .

The treatment of ageing nuns—accused of spying, though they had not left their convent since [1949]—was uncivilized and unnecessary. So too was the razing of the foreign cemetery out in the suburbs. We saw people of all ages, bound and wearing placards or the tall conical hats of shame, being marched or driven in lorries about the city. Children too young to take an active part in the movement and thus on prolonged holiday from school, were eager observers of acts of cruelty and humiliation.

1. How were people targeted by the Red Guards punished?

2. Do you think the people you read about were guilty of serious crimes?

3. What effect do you think the Cultural Revolution had on the people?

Lesson 1 Civilizations of Middle America

CLOSE READING

Civilizations Develop in the Americas

1. **Summarize** The text identifies the two main theories on how human beings migrated from Asia to the Americas. Summarize these two theories.

2. **Determine Meaning of Words** Read the section titled "Farming Begins." Based on the context, what does the term "domesticated" mean? Why was the ability to cultivate domestic plants and animals an important part of the evolution of civilization in the Americas?

The Maya

3. **Summarize** Read the section under the heading "Farming Methods." The text states that the Maya "...developed two farming methods that allowed them to thrive in the tropical environment." Summarize these two methods.

4. **Draw Inferences** How did the development of city-states contribute to the cultural advancement of the Maya?

Maya Cultural Life

5. **Determine Meaning of Words** Read the first paragraph under "Maya Cultural Life." Based on the context, what does the term "polytheistic" mean? Why is it important to know that the Maya were a polytheistic society?

6. **Draw Conclusions** Why would having a counting system be beneficial to the Maya?

The Aztec

7. **Identify Supporting Details** Read the first paragraph of "Government and Society." The text states, "War brought immense wealth as well as power to the Aztec empire." Identify details from the text that help support this statement.

8. **Compare and Contrast** Compare and contrast the Maya and Aztec civilizations. Consider topics such as religion, government, advancements in technology and understanding, and cultural innovation. Use the graphic organizer below to show how they were similar and different.

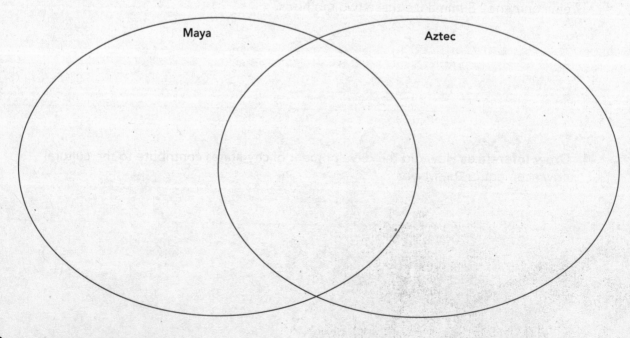

Maya   Aztec

Lesson 2 The World of the Incas

CLOSE READING

Cultures of the Andes

1. **Draw Conclusions** Why might the Moche's idea of an organized network of relay runners be adopted by later civilizations?

2. **Draw Inferences** Read the text under "Nazca, Huari, and Tiahuanaco." At the end of the last paragraph, the text states, "Many of the same artistic styles appear at Huari and Tiahuanaco, leading scholars to think that these two southern powers shared religious and trade affiliations." Based on your understanding of ancient civilizations, why would similarities in artistry lead scholars to believe that the two groups were affiliated?

The Powerful Inca Empire

3. **Draw Conclusions** The text states that the rise of the Inca emperor Pachacuti Sapa Inca was a "historic change" in Inca history. Why is the reign of Pachacuti now considered historic?

4. **Make Inferences** Why is it surprising that the Inca did not develop a system of writing?

5. **Cite Evidence** Read the text under "Uniting the Empire with Language and Roads." How did the development of language and roads help unite the Inca empire? Cite evidence from the text to support your answer.

Inca Life

6. **Summarize** How did the Inca build terraced farms, and why were terraced farms well suited to the geography in which the Inca lived?

7. **Summarize** Using the chart below, summarize the most important developments of the Inca culture. Consider advancements in government, culture and religion, agriculture, language, and engineering.

Major Advancements of the Inca	
Government	
Religion and Culture	
Agriculture	
Language	
Engineering	
Other	

Lesson 3 The Peoples of North America

CLOSE READING

Cultures Develop in the Desert Southwest

1. **Determine Meaning of Words** Read the first paragraph of "The Hohokam, Pima, and Papago." Based on the context, what does the word *irrigation* mean? Describe the Hohokam system of irrigation.

2. **Draw Conclusions** How did the environment influence the manner in which the Ancestral Puebloans built their homes?

Cultures Develop in the East

3. **Make Predictions** Look at the image of the Great Serpent Mound and read the accompanying caption. Based on this image, make a prediction about what the section entitled "The Adena and Hopewell" will cover. What kinds of questions should you ask yourself before reading the text?

4. **Draw Inferences** For what reasons might the Missisippians have built mounds on which to construct their temples?

5. **Draw Inferences** Based on what you have read, how do you think artifacts found in North America help scientists explain the lives of ancient North American civilizations? Cite evidence from the text to support your answer.

Distinct Cultures Develop in Different Geographic Regions

6. **Identify Supporting Details** What was the impact of the Iroquois League on the ancient civilizations of the Northeast? Use details from the text to support your answer.

7. **Analyze Cause and Effect** What were the effects of the natural environment on the development of ancient civilizations in North America? Fill in the chart to complete your answer.

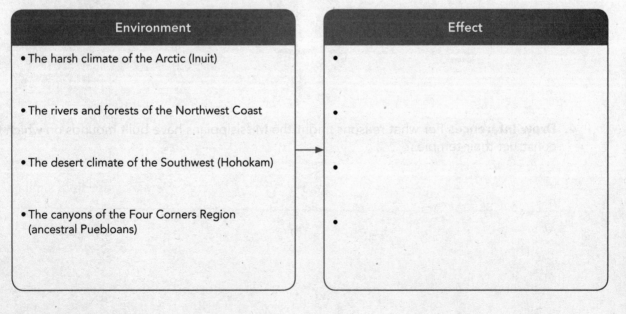

Environment	Effect
• The harsh climate of the Arctic (Inuit)	•
• The rivers and forests of the Northwest Coast	•
• The desert climate of the Southwest (Hohokam)	•
• The canyons of the Four Corners Region (ancestral Puebloans)	•

PRIMARY SOURCE EXPLORATION

Learning About the Aztecs

Introduction

Your textbook presents a lot of detail about the Aztecs and their society. But how do historians know all of this? They can't interview Moctezuma or go visit Tenochtitlan and take notes! In fact, they use four main types of sources:

1. **Aztec codices** These books were produced by indigenous people at the request of the Spanish rulers. They use indigenous pictographs and Spanish-language notes to show pre-conquest life and history.

2. **Aztec chronicles** These are records compiled by Aztec historians shortly after the Spanish conquest. They were based on earlier Aztec oral histories and other sources, and were written down in the Aztec's Nahuatl language.

3. **Spanish sources:** These include the observations of conquistadors and government officials in colonial Mexico.

4. **Archaeology:** Modern archaeologists have excavated countless artifacts that teach us about different aspects of Aztec life.

Each type of source has its own benefits and challenges. Chronicles written in Nahuatl can be difficult to translate and interpret, for example. Beautifully illustrated codices may leave out details that weren't of interest to the Spanish. In this activity you will analyze one source of each type.

Document-Based Writing Activity

Analyze the following four sources and then use information from the documents and your knowledge of world history to write an essay in which you

- Explain how historians learn about the Aztecs and their neighbors.
- Compare and contrast different sources of information about the Aztecs.

Keep in mind that your essay should include an introduction, several paragraphs, and a conclusion. In the body of the essay, use evidence from at least three documents. Support your response with relevant facts, examples, and details. In developing your essay, be sure to keep these general definitions in mind:

- *Explain* means "to make something clear by describing it."
- *Compare and contrast* means "to examine things and see how they are both similar and different."

Source 1

Codex Mendoza, 1541

This image comes from the Codex Mendoza, a document produced about 20 years after the Spanish conquest of Mexico. It includes a history of the Aztec rulers, lists of tribute paid to the Aztecs by different city-states, and information about daily life. This page shows the conquests of the Aztec ruler Chimalpopoca.

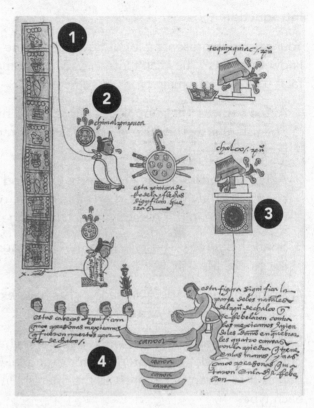

1 The bar of glyphs on the left list the years of Chimapopoca's reign. He came to power in Four Rabbit, shown at the top, and died in Thirteen Reed, at the bottom, or about 1418–1427.

2 The Aztec ruler Chimalpopoca is seated here on his reed mat, equivalent to a throne. The symbol in front of his mouth indicates speech. The shield and rising smoke behind him refer to his name, which means Smoking Shield.

3 The circular object in the box to the left is the glyph for the city-state of Chalco. The burning temple above it indicates that Chalco was defeated by Chimalpopoca.

4 The people of Chalco had rebelled against their Mexica overlords, killing five Mexica men and destroying several boats, shown here.

1. What type of accomplishments were most important for an Aztec ruler, according to this page?

2. Look at the glyph on the top right, above the glyph for Chalco. It is labelled Tequixquiac. What would you guess Tequixquiac is? Explain your answer.

3. Why might the Spanish have been interested in which city-states were once ruled by the Aztecs and how much tribute they had to pay?

Source 2

Annals of Chimalpahin, circa 1600

Chimalpahin was an indigenous historian from Chalco. Decades after the Spanish conquest, he wrote a number of historical works in Nahuatl. In the passage below, he describes an incident that occurred when Chalco was under Aztec rule. A group of musicians from Chalco went to perform for the Aztec ruler Axayacatl (ah-shah-yah-kat) to try to win better treatment for their city.

The singing and dancing began in the patio of the palace, while Axayacatl was inside with his women. The song was moving slowly. A nobleman from Tlalmanalco was playing with bad rhythm. He fainted on one of the great drums. He just drooped over the drum, not knowing how to play. And there next to the drum was standing someone named Quecholcohuatzin. He was an Amaquemecan nobleman, a great singer and drummer. When he saw that the music, the song and the dance, were to be ruined, he quickly went over to stand by the drum and began to play it, reanimating the dancing so that it wasn't ruined…

Inside, Axayacatl was listening, and when he heard how marvelously this Quecholcohuatzin played, and how he guided the singing, his heart was animated. At that he stood up, went out from where he was with his women, and went to dance. When he got to the dance floor, Axayacatl lifted up one foot, completely happy in hearing the music, and began to dance and move in circles.

When the dancing finished, the [ruler] Axayacatl said, "Greetings, my humble one! You will bring over to me the one who played and led the singing, without fail…." When Axayacatl gave this order, all the Chalca nobles were really frightened … The Chalca people thought that perhaps he was going to burn or stone the singer, the musician…

When Quecholcohuatzin arrived before Axayacatl, he kissed the earth and went on one knee, saying to him, "O lord king, may you burn me, I who am your vassal, for we have done wrong in your presence." But the [ruler] Axayacatl did not want to hear these words, saying to the ladies his women, "Women, stand up and meet him, seat him amongst you. …May your hearts be happy, o women, for what has happened. This Quecholcohuatl made me dance and sing. Never before had anyone called me forth from inside, caused me to go out and dance as he has done…"

1. What were the singers from Chalco hoping to accomplish? Do you think they were successful?

2. What did they fear? What does this say about life at the Aztec court?

3. How does Axayacatl come across in this story? How does it compare to the way rulers are depicted in the codex on the previous page?

Source 3

A True History of the Conquest of New Spain, Bernal Díaz del Castillo, 1568

Bernal Diaz del Castillo served as a soldier in the Spanish conquest of Mexico. In later life he recorded his memoirs, from which the excerpt below is taken. The conquistadors were able to witness Aztec life firsthand, but they brought their own beliefs, biases, and interests to their writings.

This excerpt describes the Spaniards' meeting with leaders of Tlaxcalla, an enemy of the Aztec empire. Remember that the ethnic group that ran the Aztec empire was called the Mexica.

He [a Tlaxcallan leader] said that Moctezuma had such great strength in warriors that when he wished to capture a great city or make a raid on a province, he could place a hundred and fifty thousand men in the field, and this they knew well from the experience of the wars and hostilities they had had with the Mexicas for more than a hundred years past.

Cortés asked: "How is it that with so many warriors which, you have said, came down on you, they have never conquered you?"

They responded: "Although the Mexicas have sometimes defeated us and killed us and carried off many of our vassals for sacrifice, many of them were also left dead on the field and others were made prisoners, and ... that all the provinces which had been raided by Moctezuma and placed under his rule were ill disposed towards the Mexicas, and that as their inhabitants were carried off by force to the wars, they did not fight with good will; indeed, it was from these very men that we received warnings, and for this reason we have defended our country to the best of our ability..."

Moreover, [another leader] said that Moctezuma kept garrisons of many warriors stationed in all the provinces in addition to the great force he could bring from the city, and that all the provinces paid tribute of gold and silver, feathers, stones, cloth and cotton, and Indian men and women for sacrifice and others for servants, that he [Moctezuma] was such a great prince that he possessed everything he could desire, that the houses where he dwelt were full of riches and [precious] stones and chalchihuites [a type of precious stone] which he had robbed and taken by force from those who would not give them willingly, and that all the wealth of the country was in his hands....

1. What weakness of the Aztecs has allowed Tlaxcalla to remain independent?

2. How do the Tlaxcallans characterize the Aztec empire?

3. Why might the Spanish have been interested in the details given by the Tlaxcallan rulers?

Source 4

Excavations at Aztec Peasant Sites, Dr. Michael E. Smith, 2003

Archaeologists have excavated sites throughout what was once the Aztec empire. The report below summarizes findings from an excavation at a rural Aztec town south of Mexico City.

The site of Cuexcomate, with 135 simple houses, was probably a rural calpolli town (a calpolli was an Aztec residential ward). In addition to the peasant houses, Cuexcomate also had a small palace, a temple, a public plaza, and a special civil building that may have been a telpochcalli school. Families at Cuexcomate and the nearby single-ward village of Capilco lived in small one-room houses with sun-dried mud brick (adobe) walls and thatched roofs. All that remains of their houses today are the wall foundations and floors that were constructed of stone. When in use, these houses probably looked much like modern adobe peasant houses....

The houses at Capilco and Cuexcomate were so small that most domestic activity probably took place in the patio outside, which was kept clear of debris. People threw their trash to the sides and rear of the house, and the study of artifacts from these locations provides information about the activities and social conditions of the families who lived in each house. Broken potsherds [pieces of pottery] from ceramic cooking pots, storage jars, serving bowls, and tortilla griddles give abundant evidence for the preparation of meals by the women of Capilco and Cuexcomate... Every house excavated at these sites also yielded ceramic spindle whorls and spinning bowls, and many had bronze sewing needles. Several types of ritual artifacts were found at all houses, including figurines and incense burners....

To judge from the nature of the artifacts found around each house, the peasants of Capilco and Cuexcomate were quite well-off economically. They were able to obtain trade goods from all over central Mexico, including obsidian from Pachuca and Otumba, salt from the Valley of Mexico, bronze goods from western Mexico, and ceramic serving bowls from the Valley of Mexico, Cholula, Toluca, Cuernavaca, and Yautepec. These imported bowls, many of them with elaborate polychrome decoration, were found in nearly all houses. The large number of imported goods suggests that the inhabitants of Capilco and Cuexcomate were able to produce sufficient crops, textiles, paper, and other goods beyond their domestic needs and tribute quotas to enter the markets as active participants.

---

1. What can archaeologists learn from the trash left outside homes by peasant families?

2. What evidence does Smith give to support his claim that the peasants of the towns he excavated were well off?

3. How does archaeology complement written sources to give historians a more complete picture of Aztec life?

Lesson 1 Early Greece

CLOSE READING

Minoans Prosper From Trade

1. **Identify Main Ideas** Use the table below to record the main ideas relating to the groups of people discussed in the lesson.

Minoans	Mycenaeans	Dorians
•	•	•
•	•	•
•	•	•

2. **Cite Evidence** Why do historians believe that Minoan women had more rights in their society than women in other ancient civilizations?

3. **Identify Central Idea** How did Minoan culture prosper?

Mycenaean Civilization

4. **Compare and Contrast** the Minoan and Mycenaean civilizations. Where and when did each civilization flourish?

5. **Summarize** How do historians know that the Trojan War actually occurred?

6. **Identify Central Idea** How did the Minoan and Mycenaean civilizations affect each other?

Homer and the Great Greek Legends

7. **Explain** What might people today learn about the ancient Greeks from the *Odyssey* and the *Iliad*?

8. **Draw Conclusions** Do you think that the epics of Homer are reliable sources of information about the history of the ancient Greeks? Why or why not?

Lesson 2 The Greek City-States

CLOSE READING

Geography Shapes Greek City-States

1. **Summarize** How did geographical features shape Greek city-states?

Discipline and Warfare in Sparta

2. **Cite Evidence** How was Sparta different from other city-states? Cite evidence from the text to support your answer.

Democracy Evolves in Athens

3. **Draw Conclusions** What were Solon's reforms in Athens? Why were many Athenians still unsatisfied with their government?

Forces for Unity

4. **Summarize** Whom did Greeks worship and how did they practice their religion?

5. **Infer** What might be some advantages and disadvantages of a society that feels superior to others?

Greek Wars with Persia

6. **Identify Key Steps in a Process** How did Greek city-states come together to defeat Persia?

Pericles, Democracy, and War

7. **Summarize** What responsibilities and privileges did citizens of Athens have during the Age of Pericles?

8. **Identify Cause and Effect** What were the cause and effects of the Peloponnesian War?

Lesson 3 Greek Thinkers, Artists, and Writers

CLOSE READING

Philosophers and the Pursuit of Wisdom

1. **Identify Supporting Details** As you read the lesson, examine the text for details that support the major ideas. Then use the graphic organizer below to record the lesson's supporting details for each topic.

Greek Civilization	
Philosophy	
Architecture and Art	
Literature	
History	

2. **Identify Central Ideas** How were the Sophists different from other philosophers of Ancient Greece?

Conveying Ideals in Architecture and Art

3. **Identify Steps in a Process** How did Greek sculpture evolve over time?

4. **Cite Evidence** How does the Parthenon convey the Greek ideas of order and harmony in the universe? Cite evidence from the text to support your answer.

Greek Literature

5. Summarize What ideas were explored in Greek tragedies?

6. Draw Conclusions Why would playwrights like Aristophanes make fun of people in their comedies?

Studying History

7. Compare and Contrast Herodotus and Thucydides.

8. Infer Why do you think research and avoiding bias is important to the study of history?

Lesson 4 Alexander the Great and the Legacy of Greece

CLOSE READING

The New Era of Alexander the Great

1. **Identify Supporting Details** As you read the lesson, make an outline similar to the one below to keep track of the important main ideas and supporting details about the empire and legacy of Alexander the Great.

> I. The New Era of Alexander the Great
>   A. Phillip II Takes Control of Greece
>   1.
>   2.
>   B. Alexander Conquers Persia.
>   1.
>   2.
> II.

2. **Identify Steps in a Process** How did Alexander come to replace Philip II?

3. **Draw Conclusions** Why do you think Alexander's soldiers refused to go east from northern India?

Alexander's Legacy

4. **Identify Central Issues** What factors shaped Hellenistic civilization?

5. **Infer** What do you think helped make Alexandria, Egypt, the greatest of Hellenistic capitals?

6. **Cite Evidence** What in the text supports the argument that women had greater freedom in the Hellenistic Age?

Hellenistic Arts and Sciences

7. **Draw Conclusions** What factors might have encouraged the tremendous growth in the arts and sciences during the Hellenistic period?

8. **Summarize** Who was Archimedes and what did he do?

PRIMARY SOURCE EXPLORATION

Women in Ancient Greek Societies

Introduction

The status of women has varied over the centuries. In some societies women have enjoyed great freedom and have wielded political power. In many other periods, restrictions on women's rights and freedoms have been severe. Over the course of ancient Greek history, women's status was constantly changing, often reflecting shifts in political power. The following sources offer a glimpse into ancient Greek women's lives over this wide span of time.

Document-Based Writing Activity

Analyze the following four sources and then use information from the documents and your knowledge of world history to write an essay in which you

- Describe how the status of women in ancient Greek societies changed over time.
- Discuss how historians use literary sources and artifacts to learn about life in ancient times.

Keep in mind that your essay should include an introduction, several paragraphs, and a conclusion. In the body of the essay, use evidence from at least three documents. Support your response with relevant facts, examples, and details. In developing your essay, be sure to keep these general definitions in mind:

- *Describe* means "to illustrate something in words or tell about it."
- *Discuss* means "to make observations about something using facts, reasoning, and argument; to present in some detail."

Source 1

Minoan Bull-leaping Fresco from Knossos, 1450 B.C.

Historians know very little about women's lives in prehistoric Greece. However, artifacts created by the Minoans suggest the presence of powerful women priestesses or rulers. This image shows two women and a man (identified by his darker skin) leaping over a bull in some kind of religious ritual.

1. What does an image of women performing athletics with men suggest about the status of women in Minoan society?

2. What clues about gender relations might the performers' costumes reveal?

3. From rodeos to Spanish bullfighting to Minoan bull-leaping, humans have always pitted their agility and wits against the ferocity of wild animals. Why do you think human beings feel compelled to do this?

Source 2

Excerpt from Medea, Euripides, 431 B.C.

During the classical period (400s–300s B.C.) women's lives were strictly controlled. Although Spartan women enjoyed some freedoms, in other city-states, respectable women were confined to their homes, "protected" by male guardians. Although we lack evidence of what women themselves thought about their predicament, male playwrights give us a glimpse of their viewpoint, as in this excerpt from the play *Medea*.

Medea: Of all things that live and have intelligence, we women are the most wretched creatures. First, we must buy a husband at a high price [providing a dowry] and take a master over our bodies, an even more painful evil than the other [Medea is claiming that men's physical control over women is an even worse evil than the high price of a dowry].

Here the stakes are highest: do we take a bad man or a good one? A woman can't get divorced and keep her good reputation, and she has no right to refuse her husband. After arriving among new customs and rules, she must be a prophet, since she was not taught at home how to deal with her husband. If we work hard at this, and our husband bears the yoke of marriage without violence, life is enviable; but, if not, better to die. A man, when he is annoyed with those inside, goes out [leaves the home] and stops the nausea in his heart, but we must look to just one person [women have to depend on her husband alone]. They say that we live lives free from danger, while they go out to fight wars with spears, but their logic is flawed. I would rather stand shield to shield [the standard Greek battle formation of this period] three times than give birth just once.

1. How does ancient Greek society regard women who have been divorced?

2. What is the worst situation that women might face in marriage? What picture does Medea give of the freedoms and restrictions of Athenian gender roles?

3. Medea gives us a hint of the argument that ancient Athenian men used to curtail women's freedom. How did men justify keeping women confined to the home?

Source 3

Excerpt from Antigone, *Sophocles, 441 B.C.*

In Sophocles' play *Antigone,* a young woman defies the laws of her uncle Creon, the king of Thebes, by performing a burial ritual for the corpse of her rebel brother. For the ancient Greeks, an unburied body was an insult to the gods and to human dignity. By burying her brother, Antigone challenges both male authority and the laws of the state.

Creon: You there, staring down at the ground, speak up: do you affirm or deny doing these things?

Antigone: I assert that I did it: I do not deny it.

Creon: . . . But, you, tell me briefly, not at length: did you know it had been announced not to do this?

Antigone: I did. Why would I not know? It was clear.

Creon: And yet you dared to overstep these laws?

Antigone: Because it wasn't Zeus who pronounced these things to me, nor did Justice, companion of the gods below, establish such laws for humanity. I would never think your pronouncements had such strength that, being mortal, they could override the unwritten, ever-lasting prescriptions of the gods, for those aren't something recently made, but live forever, and no one knows when they first appeared. I did not intend to pay the penalty to the gods for violating these laws in fear of some man's opinion, for I know I will die. How could I not, even if you had not proclaimed it? But if I die before my time, I say this is an advantage. Anyone who lives a life of sorrow as I do, how could they not count it a blessing to die? Therefore, there is no pain for me in meeting this fate, whereas if I were to endure that one born from my mother die unburied, that would cause me pain. As it is, I feel nothing. If, however, I seem to you to have acted foolishly, then perhaps I owe my foolishness to a fool.

Chorus: She's clearly the fierce daughter of a fierce father [Antigone's father was Oedipus, a strong-willed king]; she doesn't know how to bend with the wind.

Creon: . . . She showed herself capable of insolence then, going beyond the laws put before her. Her second insolence, after she had done it, was to exult in her deed and laugh that she had done it. Now I am no man, but she is a man, if power lies with her with impunity [without consequences].

1. What argument does Antigone use to justify her defiance of the laws of the state?

2. What would audiences have found shocking about Antigone's speech, at a time when women were not allowed to participate in political life?

Source 4

Idyll XV, Theocritus, c. 270 B.C.

In the Hellenistic period (323–30 B.C.), city-states lost political independence, as power shifted to kings and royal families. In this context, royal and high-born women gained more freedom of movement. Evidence of the new freedoms enjoyed by wealthier women can be found in literary works like this dialogue between two women on their way to a festival in Alexandria, Egypt during the 200s B.C.

Gorgo (*with her maid Etychis at the door, as the maid Eunoa opens it*) Praxinoa at home?

Praxinoa Dear Gorgo! at last! She is at home. I quite thought you'd forgotten me. . . . Do sit down.

Gorgo (*sitting*) O what a silly I was to come! What with the crush and the horses, Praxinoa, I've scarcely got here alive. It's all big boots and people in uniform. And the street was never-ending, and you can't think how far your house is along it.

Praxinoa That's my lunatic [Praxinoa's husband]; came and took one [a house] at the end of the world, and more an animal's den, too, than a place of a human being to live in, just to prevent you and me being neighbors, out of sheer spite, the jealous old wretch! He's always the same.

Gorgo My dear, pray don't call your good Dinon [Praxinoa's husband] such names before Baby. See how he's staring at you. (*to the child*) It's all right, Zopyrion, my pet. It's not dad-dad she's talking about.

Praxinoa Upon my word, the child understands.

Gorgo Nice dad-dad

Praxinoa And yet that dad-dad of his the other day—now I tell him "Daddy, get mother some soap and rouge [makeup] from the shop," and, would you believe it? Back he came with a packet of salt, the great six feet of folly!

Gorgo Mine's just the same. . . . But come, my dear, get your cloak and gown. I want you to come with me (*grandly*) to call on our high and might Prince Ptolemy to see the Adonis [an annual festival]. I hear the Queen's getting up something quite splendid this year. . . . (*in the street*) **Gorgo** Heavens, what a crowd! How we're to get through this awful crush and how long it's going to take us, I can't imagine. Talk of an antheap!

Praxinoa . . . Gorgo dearest! what shall we do? The Royal Horse! Don't run me down, my good man. That bay's rearing. Look, what temper! Stand back, Eunoa, you reckless girl! He'll be the death of that man. Thank goodness I left Baby at home!

1. How would you describe the social status of these women and why?

2. What incident reveals Praxinoa's confidence and lack of fear when addressing a soldier?

Lesson 1 The Roman Republic

CLOSE READING

The Rise of the Roman Civilization

1. **Integrate Information from Diverse Sources** Review the map and the text that detail Italy's location and geography. What do the text and the map indicate about the location of Rome? How do you think geography influenced the founding of Rome and its rise to power?

2. **Categorize** Create your own graphic organizer with two columns entitled **Civilization** and **Contribution.** Under the Civilization head, list three groups other than the Romans that settled in the Italian peninsula. Then, under the Contribution head, identify each group's contribution to Roman culture. Some will have more descriptive entries than others.

The Early Roman Republic

3. **Evaluate** Why was the senate a key institution in the republic? Use details from the text and illustration in your answer.

4. **Draw Conclusions** What checks and balances existed in Rome's government?

5. **Cite Evidence** What Roman political ideas formed the foundation of many modern democratic governments?

Roman Society

6. **Draw Inferences** Why do you think the Romans believed that it was important to educate both male and female children? Consider the role of citizens in the republic when writing your answer.

7. **Summarize** After reading this text, go back to your graphic organizer and revise it to include more information about Greek contributions to Roman culture.

The Roman Republic Expands

8. **Determine Central Ideas** What attributes of Roman rule helped it maintain control over the land and people it conquered?

9. **Draw Conclusions** Why were Roman citizen-soldiers steadfast in their devotion to the republic? Explain how this may have aided Roman conquest.

10. **Compare and Contrast** What were the rights and responsibilities of citizens and non-citizens in the Roman republic?

Lesson 2 The Roman Empire: Rise and Decline

CLOSE READING

Empire Building Through Conquest

1. **Summarize** How did Rome's conquests affect the empire?

2. **Analyze Interactions** What caused the three Punic Wars between Rome and Carthage?

The Roman Republic Declines

3. **Determine Central Issues** What sparked the infighting that eventually led to the decline of Rome's republic?

4. **Summarize** What did Caesar accomplish as dictator?

The Roman Empire

5. **Determine Central Ideas** What fundamental institutions established by Augustus are still used today?

The Roman Empire Splits

6. Categorize What economic and social issues disturbed the balance of the empire?

7. Identify Supporting Details How did political turmoil affect the stability of the Roman empire?

Rome Faces Invasions

8. Draw Conclusions How did the Huns and other invaders weaken the Roman empire?

Why Did Rome Fall?

9. Analyze Word Choices What is inaccurate about the phrase "the fall of Rome"?

10. Identify Supporting Details Explain how the Germanic takeover affected Roman customs and language. What parts of the Roman civilization were preserved?

Lesson 3 The Legacy of Rome

CLOSE READING

Roman Literature, History, and Philosophy

1. **Cite Evidence** Reread this quote from the Roman poet Horace. "Greece has conquered her rude conqueror." Do you agree with his statement? Cite examples to support your opinion.

2. **Compare and Contrast** How did Romans use literature to influence people? Consider their methods and goals when writing your answer.

3. **Determine Author's Point of View** Reread Livy's passage on the importance of studying history. In what ways does he say we can learn from history? What do you think Livy's motivation was in writing his heroic tales?

Roman Art, Architecture, and Drama

4. **Summarize** What did Roman sculptors try to accomplish in their art?

5. **Use Visual Information** Look at the image of the mosaic from Pompeii. What does this show you about daily life in ancient Rome?

6. **Identify Supporting Details** What two famous Roman buildings are covered in the lesson? How do they provide evidence of the diffusion of Roman ideas?

Roman Achievements in Science and Engineering

7. **Draw Conclusions** What evidence supports the idea that Romans perfected their engineering skills?

Roman Law Unites the Empire

8. **Summarize** Identify the Roman principles that are the foundation for the American legal system.

9. **Cite Evidence** Why were Romans not truly equal before the law?

Lesson 4 The Origins of Christianity

CLOSE READING

Romans Accept Many Religions

1. Summarize What were some of the religions in the early empire, and what does this diversity reveal about the Roman empire?

2. Identify Cause and Effect As you read "Divisions in Judea" and "Rome Crushes the Jewish Revolt," use this graphic organizer to record the causes and effects of the Jewish revolt against Rome.

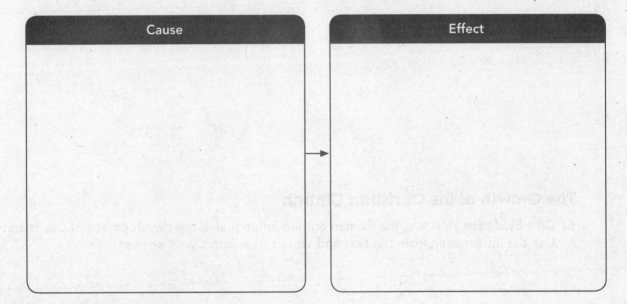

Cause	Effect

The Teachings of Jesus

3. Determine Central Ideas Describe the central ideas of Christianity.

4. **Draw Conclusions** What is significant about the fact that Jesus emphasized mercy, sympathy, and forgiveness? Consider what you have read about the Roman empire. Why might the emphasis on these qualities appeal to many of his followers?

Christianity Spreads

5. **Use Visual Information** Look at the map of the Spread of Christianity to A.D. 476. Use information from the map to write a summary that describes the spread of Christianity.

The Growth of the Christian Church

6. **Cite Evidence** How was the Roman empire influential in the development of Christianity? Use the information from the text and visuals to support your answer.

PRIMARY SOURCE EXPLORATION

Augustus Caesar: Benevolent Ruler or Tyrant?

Introduction

Octavian was nineteen when he became a driving force in Roman politics. Adopted nephew of Julius Caesar, he became part of the triumvirate that ruled after Caesar's assassination. The triumvirs defeated Caesar's assassins, then turned on each other. Octavian emerged as the final victor in the struggle for power. For more than 40 years, he ruled as Augustus Caesar – the first Roman emperor. But what kind of ruler was he?

Document-Based Writing Activity

Analyze the following four sources and then use information from the documents and your knowledge of world history to write an essay in which you

- Describe the accomplishments of Augustus Caesar.
- Explain why he has been both admired and condemned.

Keep in mind that your essay should include an introduction, several paragraphs, and a conclusion. In the body of the essay, use evidence from at least three documents. Support your response with relevant facts, examples, and details. In developing your essay, be sure to keep these general definitions in mind:

- *Describe* means "to illustrate something in words or tell about it."
- *Explain* means "to make plain or understandable; to give reasons for or causes of; or to show the logical development or relationships of."

Source 1

The Deeds of the Divine Augustus, circa A.D. 14

Toward the end of his long reign, Augustus wrote a long account of his accomplishments as emperor of Rome. In his will, he instructed the Senate to post *The Deeds of the Divine Augustus* on two bronze pillars outside his tomb. Following are some excerpts from the long inscription.

A copy below of the deeds of the divine Augustus, by which he subjected the whole wide earth to the rule of the Roman people, and of the money which he spent for the state and Roman people, inscribed on two bronze pillars, which are set up in Rome.

- In my nineteenth year, on my own initiative and at my own expense, I raised an army with which I set free the state, which was oppressed by the domination of a faction.... I often waged war, civil and foreign, on the earth and sea, in the whole wide world, and as victor I spared all the citizens who sought pardon. . . .

- Twenty one times I was named emperor. When the senate decreed more triumphs for me, I sat out from all of them.... When the dictatorship was offered to me, both in my presence and my absence, by the people and senate, when Marcus Marcellus and Lucius Arruntius were consuls, I did not accept it. . . .

- When my sons Gaius and Lucius Caesar, whom fortune stole from me as youths, were fourteen, the senate and Roman people made them consuls-designate on behalf of my honor, so that they would enter that magistracy after five years....

- I paid to the Roman plebs, HS 300 per man from my father's will and in my own name gave HS 400 from the spoils of war when I was consul for the fifth time.... I paid out rewards in cash to the soldiers whom I had led into their towns when their service was completed, and in this venture I spent about HS 400,000,000. . . .

- Three times I gave shows of gladiators under my name and five times under the name of my sons and grandsons; in these shows about 10,000 men fought. Twice I furnished under my name spectacles of athletes gathered from everywhere, and three times under my grandson's name. . . .

- I restored peace to the sea from pirates. In that slave war I handed over to their masters for the infliction of punishments about 30,000 captured, who had fled their masters and taken up arms against the state. . . .

---

1. Which of the deeds listed here would have won great approval from members of the Roman army? From landowners? From merchants? From ordinary Roman citizens?

2. How does Augustus appeal to Roman pride and patriotism?

3. Would you consider this a reliable source of information? Why or why not?

Source 2

Images of Augustus Caesar

There are probably more surviving images of Augustus Caesar than of any other figure of the ancient world. Many of them are on Roman coins issued by his treasury. These images give us a clear picture of how Augustus wanted himself to be seen.

This coin depicts Augustus wearing the Civic Crown, a wreath of oak leaves awarded to soldiers who saved the lives of other Roman citizens. It was awarded to Augustus for his role in ending the civil wars.

This 7-foot marble statue of Augustus was found at a villa owned by his third wife. It is believed to be a copy of a bronze original, now lost, displayed in Rome during his lifetime.

1. Why do you think Augustus wanted coins issued that showed him wearing the Civic Crown?

2. What impression of Augustus do you get from the statue?

3. In the United States, it is illegal to issue coins or stamps showing living people. Why do you think that is?

Source 3

The Annals, Tacitus, circa A.D. 116

One of the greatest Roman historians, Tacitus was a senator and a great admirer of the Roman Republic. In his final work, the *Annals*, Tacitus described the history of the empire in the years following the death of Augustus.

Augustus won over the soldiers with gifts, the populace with cheap corn, and all men with the sweets of repose, and so grew greater by degrees, while he concentrated in himself the functions of the Senate, the magistrates, and the laws. He was wholly unopposed, for the boldest spirits had fallen in battle, or in the proscription, while the remaining nobles, the readier they were to be slaves, were raised the higher by wealth and promotion, so that, [made rich] by revolution, they preferred the safety of the present to the dangerous past. Nor did the provinces dislike that condition of affairs, for they distrusted the government of the Senate and the people, because of the rivalries between the leading men and the rapacity of the officials, while the protection of the laws was unavailing, as they were continually deranged by violence, intrigue, and finally by corruption.

Augustus meanwhile, as supports to his despotism, raised to [high office] Claudius Marcellus, his sister's son, while a mere stripling, and Marcus Agrippa, of humble birth, a good soldier, and one who had shared his victory, to two consecutive consulships. . . .

At home all was tranquil, and there were magistrates with the same titles; there was a younger generation, sprung up since the victory of Actium, and even many of the older men had been born during the civil wars. How few were left who had seen the republic!

Thus the State had been revolutionized, and there was not a vestige left of the old sound morality. Stript of equality, all looked up to the commands of a sovereign without the least apprehension for the present, while Augustus in the vigor of life, could maintain his own position, that of his house, and the general tranquility. When in advanced old age, he was worn out by a sickly frame, and the end was near and new prospects opened, a few spoke in vain of the blessings of freedom, but most people dreaded and some longed for war. The popular gossip of the large majority fastened itself variously on their future masters.

---

1. According to Tacitus, why did Augustus win widespread support in Rome?

2. What differences does Tacitus see between Rome before and after the reign of Augustus?

3. Would you consider this a reliable source of information? Why or why not?

Source 4

Augustus, First Emperor of Rome, *Adrian Goldsworthy, 2014*

In a recent biography of Augustus Caesar, English historian Adrian Goldsworthy explored the life and legacy of the first Roman emperor. Here, he discusses how the reputation of Augustus varied in his own time and in later centuries.

You cannot study Roman history without coming across Augustus and his legacy. He was the first emperor, the man who finally replaced a Republic which had lasted for almost half a millennium with a veiled monarchy. The system he created gave the empire some 250 years of stability, when it was both larger and more prosperous than at any other time. . . .

The great-nephew of the murdered Julius Caesar, he was made the principal heir in his will and given his name, which he took to mean full adoption. Power was not supposed to be inherited at Rome, but armed with his name, he rallied the dead dictator's supporters and proclaimed his intention to assume all of his father's offices and status.... The young, murderous warlord of the civil wars then managed to reinvent himself as the beloved guardian of the state, took the name 'Augustus' with its religious overtones, and was eventually dubbed 'the father of his country'...

Julius Caesar has often attracted fawning adulation and bitter loathing, and the same is almost as true of Augustus. Throughout the nineteenth century and beyond, he was widely praised for curing the malaise of a broken republic, giving the Romans peace, stability, and prosperity as a benevolent monarch. In an era when kings and empires still dominated Europe and much of the world, such an understanding came readily. . . .

The modern world has grown very suspicious of dictators of whatever political hue, and less willing to pardon the murderous nature of Augustus' rise as being justified by the peace he eventually created. Yet we need to be careful not to paint the past in simple shades, or automatically to assume that all dictators and all empires, or indeed all states, are essentially alike. Augustus killed a lot of people, but he inflicted on the world nothing like the misery of a Hitler or a Stalin, and, as ever, we should view his behavior in the context of the times. In his willingness to kill his enemies he was no better or worse than the other warlords to appear at that time.

1. How does Goldsworthy describe the major impact of Augustus on Rome?

2. According to Goldsworthy, how did Augustus Caesar shape his own image?

3. Why does Goldsworthy think that people today are more likely to judge Augustus harshly than people in the past?

Lesson 1 The Early Middle Ages

CLOSE READING

The Byzantine Empire Thrives

1. **Integrate Information from Diverse Sources** Read the first two paragraphs of "Constantinople Grows." Then look at the map of Constantinople. What do the text and the map convey about Constantinople? What different information about Constantinople can you draw from both sources?

The Age of Justinian

2. **Summarize** Why was Justinian's reform of the law so important? Use evidence from the text to support your answer.

3. **Draw Inferences** Why do you think that the Byzantine empire had a healthy money economy, while in Western Europe the use of money declined? Use evidence from the text to support your answer.

Changes in Western Europe *and* Germanic Kingdoms

4. **Identify Supporting Details** Read the text of "Changes in Western Europe" and "Germanic Kingdoms." The first paragraph of "Germanic Kingdoms" states that the culture of the Germanic tribes differed greatly from Rome's culture. List details from the text that support this assertion.

Charlemagne Builds an Empire

5. **Analyze Interactions** What do you think Pope Leo III and Charlemagne each thought about crowning a Germanic king as successor to the Roman emperors? Cite text details to discuss how this event might affect each of them.

6. **Identify Key Steps in a Process** What important actions did Charlemagne undertake to reunite Europe? Support your answer with details from the text.

New Invasions Pound Europe

7. **Summarize** What legacy did Charlemagne leave to future Europeans? Reference details from the text to support your answer.

8. **Compare and Contrast** How were the waves of invaders that threatened Europe after Charlemagne's death similar to and different from each other? Support your answer by citing details from the text and map.

Lesson 2 Feudalism and the Manor Economy

CLOSE READING

Feudalism Develops

1. **Identify Cause and Effect** In what ways did the waves of invasions by Vikings, Muslims, and Magyars affect the people of medieval Europe? Support your response with details from the text.

2. **Categorize** Which obligations do you think were the most important to lords? To vassals? Reference details from the text to support your answer.

3. **Draw Inferences** How could a vassal holding fiefs from more than one lord deal with conflicts arising from quarrels between his lords?

Nobles, Knights, and Warfare

4. **Identify Supporting Details** What do you think is significant about the fact that "powerful lords fortified their homes to withstand attack" during the early Middle Ages?

5. **Draw Conclusions** Why do you think that "few real knights could live up to the ideals of chivalry"? Cite evidence from the text to support your conclusions.

Manorialism

6. **Use Visual Information** Look at the illustration of the medieval manor. How do details shown in the illustration support the statement that "the manor was generally self-sufficient"?

7. **Summarize** What was daily life on a manor like for peasants during the Middle Ages? What were some of the ways it varied with the season? Use evidence from the text to support your answer.

Lesson 3 The Medieval Christian Church

CLOSE READING

The Church Shapes Everyday Life

1. **Identify Supporting Details** How did religion play a vital role in medieval life? As you read this section, use the chart to identify the main ideas for all the subheadings in the section.

The Spread of Christianity	The Parish Priest	The Village Church	The Rise of Cathedrals	Women and the Church

2. **Draw Conclusions** Read the text under "Women and the Church." How do you think Church teachings about women influenced people's daily lives?

Life in Monasteries and Convents

3. **Draw Inferences** Monasteries provided education to some children who would not otherwise have had the opportunity to attend school. How do you think monastic schools might have helped spread Christianity across Europe?

The Growth of Church Power

4. Draw Conclusions How did the Church's spiritual authority lead to political power?

The Church Faces Calls to Reform

5. Identify Cause and Effect How did the success of the Church lead to problems and calls for reform?

Jewish Communities in Medieval Europe

6. Identify Cause and Effect What led Jews to migrate to Eastern Europe and Muslim lands?

The Christian Church Is Divided

7. Compare and Contrast Explain how the Roman Church and Byzantine Church were similar and different.

Lesson 4 Economic Expansion and Change: The Crusades and After

CLOSE READING

Changes in Agriculture Transform Europe

1. **Identify Cause and Effect** Use this graphic organizer to record *causes* and *effects* of the population growth in medieval Europe from 1000 to 1300.

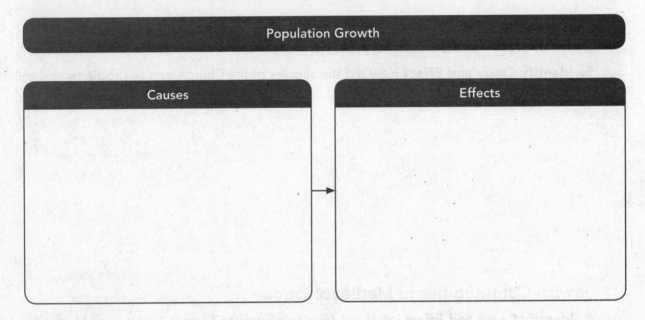

Population Growth

Causes	Effects

Trade Expands and Towns Grow

2. **Synthesize** How did the growing middle class lead to the expansion of towns and cities?

Economic Changes

3. **Draw Conclusions** Why did merchants use letters of credit and bills of exchange?

A New Middle Class

4. **Make Inferences** Why did guilds develop?

5. **Cite Evidence** How does the text show that women benefited as a result of the growth of the middle class?

The Crusades

6. **Identify Supporting Details** Why did Pope Urban II agree to help Byzantine emperor Alexius I?

The Effects of the Crusades

7. **Cite Evidence** How did the Crusades further encourage the growth of a money economy?

The Reconquista

8. **Draw Conclusions** What effect did Isabella's desire for unity have on Spain?

Lesson 5 The Feudal Monarchs and the Church

CLOSE READING

Feudal Monarchs Begin to Centralize Power

1. **Determine Central Ideas** As you read the lesson, use this table to record the events or actions that affected the power of the monarchies in each nation.

	Relations with Church Increased Monarch's Power	Relations with Church Contained Monarch's Power
England		
France		
Holy Roman Empire		

English Kings Expand Their Power

2. **Cite Evidence** Why was Henry II an important king in English history? Cite evidence from the text in your answer.

Developing New Traditions of Government

3. **Draw Inferences** How did Parliament help unify England?

Growth of the French Monarchy

4. Compare and Contrast What are some of the similarities and some of the differences between the development of the French monarchy and the development of the English monarchy?

The Holy Roman Empire

5. Draw Inferences What institution were some of the officials that Otto I appointed to government positions connected with? What did that mean about who had power in Otto's government?

A Pope and an Emperor Feud

6. Summarize What was the cause of the feud between Henry IV and Pope Gregory VII? Why was this feud important?

The Battle for Italy

7. Use Visual Information Look at the map titled "The Holy Roman Empire, 1300s." Describe what it shows and explain why the area shown developed in this way.

Church Power Reaches Its Peak

8. Determine Author's Purpose What did Pope Innocent III mean when he said that the pope is "between God and man, lower than God but higher than men, who judges all and is judged by no one"?

Lesson 6 Learning, Literature, and the Arts of the Middle Ages

CLOSE READING

The Rise of Medieval Universities

1. **Identify Cause and Effect** What conditions caused the expansion of education during the High Middle Ages?

2. **Compare and Contrast** Use the graphic organizer to record the similarities and differences between higher education in the High Middle Ages and higher education today.

Similar to today	Different from today

3. **Determine Author's Point of View** Read the excerpt below and describe the author's point of view. How was it similar to the views of most people of the time? How was it different?

   "If it were customary to send daughters to school like sons, and if they were then taught the same subjects, they would learn as thoroughly and understand the subtleties of all arts and sciences as well as sons."

New Knowledge Reaches Europe

4. **Summarize** Why did science make few advancements in Western Europe during this period? How did some scientists try to resolve this problem?

Medieval Literature

5. **Compare and Contrast** Think about Dante's *Divine Comedy* and Chaucer's *Canterbury Tales.* What does each work tell us about medieval life?

Architecture and Art

6. **Determine Central Ideas** What was the purpose of the Gothic style of architecture? Discuss elements of Gothic architecture in your answer.

7. **Draw Conclusions** How did medieval European architecture and art reflect the importance of religion in medieval life?

The Byzantine Heritage

8. **Summarize** In what ways did Byzantine culture influence other peoples?

Lesson 7 The Late Middle Ages: A Time of Upheaval

CLOSE READING

The Black Death Spreads Across Europe

1. **Explain an Argument** By 1347, trade with other parts of the world was becoming more common. This expansion of trade was both one of the best and worst things that happened to Europe in the late Middle Ages. Explain why this statement is a valid argument.

2. **Identify Supporting Details** What details under "Social Upheaval" support the idea that "terror and bewilderment" can cause people to respond in unusual or illogical ways?

3. **Summarize** How did the Black Death cause economic upheaval?

Crisis in the Church

4. **Draw Inferences** How did the pope's move to Avignon and the establishment of rival popes encourage reformers?

The Hundred Years' War

5. **Identify Cause and Effect** What were the sources of conflict between the English and French at the beginning of the Hundred Years' War?

6. **Analyze Interactions** Aside from Joan of Arc's belief that she was on a holy mission, what are the possible reasons that she, as a teenage peasant girl with no military experience, was able to inspire and lead entire French armies of hardened soldiers?

7. **Identify Key Steps in a Process** What was the process by which England's Parliament won the "power of the purse" by the end of the Hundred Years' War?

8. **Draw Conclusions** How did the introduction of war weapons, such as the longbow and cannon, affect medieval society?

Lesson 8 Russia and Eastern Europe

CLOSE READING

The Geography of Russia

1. **Summarize** Use this graphic organizer to help you take notes for a summary of why Russia developed differently from Western Europe during the medieval period.

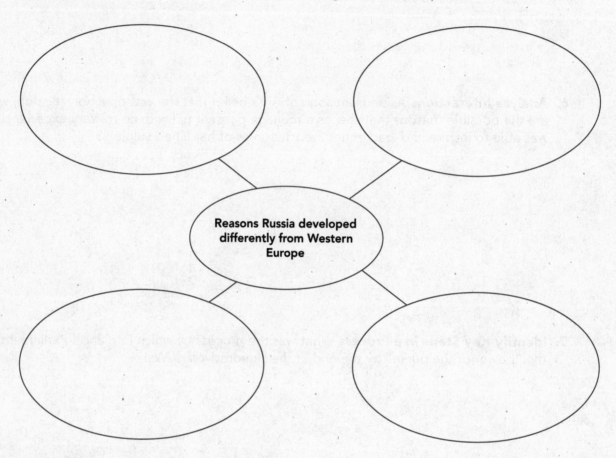

Reasons Russia developed differently from Western Europe

Early Russia

2. **Identify Cause and Effect** How did Russia's ties with the Byzantine empire influence the relationship between church and state?

The Mongols Conquer Russia

3. **Make Inferences** Why did the Mongol rulers of Russia tolerate the Russian Orthodox Church?

Moscow Surpasses Kiev

4. Draw Conclusions How did Moscow become the center of power in Russia?

The Geography of Eastern Europe

5. Categorize What were the main influences on the different regions of Eastern Europe?

Migrations Increase Diversity

6. Summarize How did outside cultural influences affect religious diversity in different regions of Eastern Europe?

7. Make Inferences Why did Eastern Europe become a refuge for many Jews?

Early Kingdoms of Eastern Europe

8. Analyze Interactions What event ended Hungarian independence in 1526?

PRIMARY SOURCE EXPLORATION

Murder at Canterbury Cathedral

Introduction

A medieval tug-of-war between the Roman Catholic Church and various monarchs spanned centuries as popes and kings struggled for power in Europe. The murder of Archbishop Thomas Becket in 1170 plays a pivotal role in this tale of dominance and intrigue. The archbishop and England's King Henry II had been fighting for years. The latest chapter in their disagreement involved two main issues. The king had issued the Constitutions of Clarendon in 1164 in a bid to reduce the power of the Church. Becket, however, refused to observe them. Then the archbishop excommunicated three bishops who supported the king. On learning of the excommunications, Henry is reported to have exclaimed that "among all those he maintained . . . he had none that would vindicate him from one Priest that troubled him." Henry was referring, of course, to the archbishop. Hearing his exclamation, four of the king's knights hastened to Canterbury, determined to deal with this troublesome priest. On the night of December 29, 1170, as evening prayers were being sung at the Cathedral, the knights burst onto the scene and murdered Becket. This event echoed down through the ages and influenced the ongoing power struggle between Church and state.

Document-Based Writing Activity

Analyze the following four sources and then use information from the documents and your knowledge of medieval European history to write an essay in which you

- Explain how the murder of the archbishop affected the power struggle between the Church and the English monarchy.
- Discuss how these sources show the entanglement of Church and state during this time period, referencing specific sources in your answer.

Keep in mind that your essay should include an introduction, several paragraphs, and a conclusion. In the body of the essay, use evidence from at least three documents. Support your response with relevant facts, examples, and details. In developing your essay, be sure to keep these general definitions in mind:

- *Explain* means "to make plain or understandable; to give reasons for or causes of; or to show the logical development or relationships of."
- *Discuss* means "to make observations about something using facts, reasoning, and argument; to present in some detail."

Source 1

The Life of Saint Thomas, Archbishop of Canterbury and Martyr, Edward Grim, 1173

Edward Grim, a visitor to Canterbury Cathedral, was with Archbishop Thomas Becket when he was murdered. Grim himself was wounded as he attempted to protect Becket. He later wrote about the attack.

. . . the sacrilegious men entered the house of peace and reconciliation with swords drawn; indeed the sight alone as well as the rattle of arms inflicted not a small amount of horror on those who watched. And those knights who approached the confused and disordered people who had been observing vespers [evening prayer] but, by now, had run toward the lethal spectacle exclaimed in a rage: "Where is Thomas Becket, traitor of the king and kingdom?" No one responded and instantly they cried out more loudly, "Where is the archbishop?" Unshaken he . . . said in an adequately audible voice, "Here I am, not a traitor of the king but a priest; why do you seek me?" . . . The murderers pursued him and asked, "Absolve and restore to communion those you have excommunicated and return to office those who have been suspended." To these words [Thomas] replied, "No penance [action showing regret] has been made, so I will not absolve them." "Then you," they said, "will now die and will suffer what you have earned." "And I," he said, "am prepared to die for my Lord, so that in my blood the church will attain liberty and peace; but in the name of Almighty God I forbid that you hurt my men. . . ."

With rapid motion they laid sacrilegious hands on him, handling and dragging him roughly outside of the walls of the church. . . . [H]e bravely pushed one [of the knights] . . . saying, "Don't touch me, Reginald, you who owes me faith and obedience, you who foolishly follow your accomplices." On account of the rebuff the knight was suddenly set on fire with a terrible rage and, wielding a sword . . . said, "I don't owe faith or obedience to you that is in opposition to the fealty [faithfulness] I owe my lord king." The invincible martyr—seeing that the hour which would bring the end to his miserable mortal life was at hand . . . with his neck bent as if he were in prayer and with his joined hands elevated above—commended himself and the cause of the Church to God, St. Mary, and the blessed martyr St. Denis.

1. What demand did the knights make of the archbishop? Why?

2. What did the archbishop mean when he said "in my blood the church will attain liberty and peace"?

3. In what way does the conversation in the second paragraph echo the ongoing struggle between the Roman Catholic Church and the English monarchy?

Source 2

The Church Historians of England, William of Newburgh, c. 1200

Many people believed that the king had ordered the murder of the archbishop. This fact led to considerable alarm in the Church. For his part, Henry had to decide how to handle the situation. Below, the historian William of Newburgh relates how it all unfolded.

Whilst almost all persons then attributed the death of this holy man to the king, . . . the king sent representatives to Rome, to mitigate [make less severe], by submissive entreaty [pleading; pleas], the displeasure which was raging against him. When they arrived at Rome . . . it was with difficulty that they were admitted. Constantly affirming, however, that this dreadful outrage was not committed either by the command or concurrence of their master, they, at length, obtained that [a representative] from the pope, vested with full power, should be sent into France, who, on carefully investigating, and ascertaining the truth of the matter, should admit the king either to the purgation of his fame [that is, to free him of the negative attention he had received for his alleged role in the murder], or punish him, if found guilty, by ecclesiastical [Church] censure [a formal condemnation], which was done accordingly. For two cardinals being dispatched from the holy see . . . they arrived in France; and a solemn meeting being summoned in the territory of the king of England, consisting of prelates and nobles, they formally undertook the purgation of this same prince; there, humbly making his appearance, and firmly protesting that what had sullied his fame had taken place without his wish or command, and that he had never been so much afflicted with any transaction before. Indeed, he did not deny that those murderers had, perhaps, taken occasion and daring to their excessive fury from some words of his too incautiously uttered; when, hearing of the suspension of the prelates [the excommunication of the bishops by Thomas Becket], he became infuriated, and spake [spoke] unadvisedly. "And, on this account," said he, "I do not refuse the discipline of the Church: I will submit devotedly to whatever you decree, and I will fulfil your injunction." . . . The cardinals, overjoyed at the humility of so great a prince, and weeping with joy, while numbers joined their tears, and gave praise to God, dissolved the assembly, - the king's conscience being quieted, and his character in some measure restored.

---

1. What was the pope's reaction to the murder of Thomas Becket? How do you know this?

2. What did King Henry do after learning of the archbishop's murder? What does this imply?

3. What is the king's answer to the charge that he was responsible for the murder?

Source 3

The Martyrdom of Saint Thomas Becket, Willem Vrelant, early 1460s

A martyr is a person who is killed because of his or her religious beliefs. Thomas Becket became a martyr when he was murdered in 1170. People began making pilgrimages to his tomb and he was made a saint in 1173. Images of Archbishop Becket and his murder were soon seen across Europe, in illuminated manuscripts, stained glass windows, sculptures, shrines, and other depictions.

1. Who is the figure in the center of this painting? How can you tell?

This illuminated manuscript was painted in Bruges, Belgium.

2. How do the details of this painting compare with Edward Grim's description of events in Source 1?

3. What inference can you make based on the date of this illuminated manuscript?

Source 4

The Proclamation of Henry VIII, 1538

King Henry VIII was determined to win the battle against the Church for ultimate authority in England. In 1538, he declared Becket unsainted and had his shrine demolished.

. . . for as much as it appeareth now clearly, that . . . his [Archbishop Thomas Becket's] death, which they untruly called martyrdom, happened upon a rescue by him made, and that, as it is written, he gave opprobrious [scornful] words to the gentlemen. . . . And he . . . took Tracy [one of the four knights] by the bosom, and violently shook and plucked him in such manner, that he had almost overthrown him to the pavement of the Church; so that upon this fray [fight] one of their company, perceiving the same, struck him, and so in the throng Becket was slain. . . .

Following the proclamation, Saint Thomas's name was erased from or cut out of many books, including this illuminated manuscript from Belgium.

For these and for other great and urgent causes, long to recite, the King's Majesty, by the advice of his council, hath thought expedient to declare to his loving subjects, that notwithstanding the said canonization, there appeareth nothing in his life and exterior conversation, whereby he should be called a saint, but rather esteemed to have been a rebel and traitor to his prince [King Henry II]. Therefore his Grace straightly chargeth and commandeth that from henceforth the said Thomas Becket shall not be esteemed, named, reputed, nor called a saint, but bishop Becket; and that his images and pictures, through the whole realm, shall be put down, and avoided out of all churches, chapels, and other places; and that from henceforth, the days used to be festival in his name shall not be observed, nor the . . . prayers, in his name read, but razed [destroyed] and put out of all the books. . . .

---

1. According to King Henry VIII, how did Thomas Becket die?

2. How does this compare to the other accounts of the archbishop's death?

3. Why do you think King Henry VIII was threatened by the people's devotion to St. Thomas?

Lesson 1 The Origins of Islam

CLOSE READING

Muhammad and Early Islam

1. **Draw Conclusions** How does the meaning of the word *Islam* (submission to God) fit Muhammad's life?

2. **Categorize** Why are Mecca and Medina the most important cities for Muslims?

Teachings of Islam

3. **Determine Central Ideas** Fill out the chart below, providing each of the Pillars of Islam and explaining why they are important to Muslims.

Pillar of Islam	Significance
1.	1.
2.	2.
3.	3.
4.	4.
5.	5.

4. **Summarize** In addition to shared religious beliefs, how has Islam helped unite Muslims from many regions?

Islam as a Way of Life

5. **Compare and Contrast** How do the Quran and Sharia guide Muslims?

6. **Cite Evidence** How did early Islam affect the lives of women?

7. **Draw Inferences** Which aspects of Islam would have appealed to the poor, enslaved, and isolated?

Lesson 2 A Muslim Empire

CLOSE READING

Islam Faces Challenges

1. **Summarize** How did the early Muslim leaders help Muslims deal with Muhammad's death?

2. **Evaluate Explanations** How did the unity of the Arabs affect the balance of power in the Middle East, North Africa, and Europe?

Divisions Split Islam

3. **Make Inferences** What are some possible outcomes of the schism (division) between the Sunni and Shiite Muslims?

Umayyad Caliphs Create an Arab Empire

4. **Evaluate Explanations** How did the early Muslim leaders' treatment of non-Muslims help them avoid conflict?

5. Identify Supporting Ideas Identify two reasons for the decline of the Umayyad empire and explain why these two reasons helped bring down the caliphate.

New Rule Under the Abbasid Dynasty

6. Compare and Contrast How was the Abbasids' treatment of non-Muslims similar to that of the Umayyads? How was it different?

7. Summarize Why was Baghdad a special place under the Abbasids?

Decline of the Arab Empire

8. Cause and Effect Why did the Abbasid caliphate decline and eventually break up?

Lesson 3 Achievements of Muslim Civilization

CLOSE READING

Economic and Social Changes

1. **Determine Author's Point of View** Does the quote from the "Sayings of the Prophet" have a positive or negative view of merchants? Give evidence to support your answer.

2. **Summarize** Why did agriculture thrive in the Muslim empires?

3. **Explain** How could enslaved people become free under Abbasid rule?

Literature, Art, and Architecture

4. **Draw Inferences** How would the prohibition on depicting humans or God in illustrations make Islamic art different from European art?

5. **Use Context Clues** Read the text under "A Rich Tradition of Literature." What would a "worldly" topic be?

6. **Determine Author's Purpose** What does the quote from *The Rubáiyát* by Omar Khayyám mean?

An Emphasis on Knowledge

7. **Draw Inferences** Why was it important for Muslim scholars to preserve the learning of earlier civilizations?

8. **Identify Supporting Details** Name three ways in which Islamic physicians broke new ground.

Lesson 4 The Ottoman and Safavid Empires

CLOSE READING

Growth of the Ottoman Empire

1. **Integrate Information From Diverse Sources** Which details in the text help to explain how the Ottomans were able to conquer Constantinople?

2. **Use Visual Information** Refer to the Ottoman and Safavid Empires map and find Vienna on the map. Why would it be difficult to stage an assault on Vienna from the Ottoman capital of Istanbul, and why was Vienna a strategic position for the rest of Europe?

3. **Identify Cause and Effect** How did conquering Constantinople help the Ottomans control trade between Asia and Europe?

Ottoman Society

4. **Draw Conclusions** How does Suleiman's nickname of "The Lawgiver" and his establishment of a vast bureaucracy indicate one of the main reasons why the Ottoman empire lasted as long as it did without weakening?

5. **Draw Inferences** The Ottoman empire recruited officers and government officials from the populations of conquered lands rather than just from the people of its core territory. How was this a benefit to the Ottoman empire?

6. **Compare and Contrast** the events that led to the rise and fall of the Ottoman empire. Reference details from the text to support your answer.

The Rise of the Safavids

7. **Summarize** What role did geography and religion play in the continuing pressures on the Safavid empire?

8. **Determine Central Ideas** What was a lasting legacy of the Safavid empire?

Lesson 5 Early Civilizations of Africa

CLOSE READING

The Geography of Africa

1. **Draw Inferences** How might Africa's vast mineral resources, including salt, gold, and iron, have caused the growth of Africa's trading cities?

Migration of People and Ideas

2. **Determine Central Ideas** How did the desertification of Northern Africa impact the movement of people and ideas?

3. **Summarize** Why did Neolithic villages thrive in the Sahara?

4. **Explain** How did the Bantu migration contribute to Africa's rich diversity of cultures?

Egypt and Nubia Flourish

5. **Cite Evidence** What natural resources allowed Nubia to manufacture tools and weapons?

6. **Draw Conclusions** How might Nubia's success have led to its downfall?

North Africa in the Ancient World

7. **Identify Cause and Effect** How did Rome's defeat of Carthage impact Northern Africa?

8. **Determine Central Ideas** How did Muslim Arabs change the cultural and religious landscape of early Africa?

Lesson 6 Kingdoms of West Africa

CLOSE READING

Trade Grows Across the Sahara

1. **Analyze Interactions** Explain why salt was the most important trading commodity in the Sahara.

Ghana

2. **Identify Key Steps** What aspects of the gold and salt trade facilitated Ghana's rise as a prosperous kingdom?

3. **Analyze Interactions** How did Islam impact Ghana's government?

Mali

4. **Draw Conclusions:** How did Mansa Musa ensure prosperity in Mali?

5. **Draw Inferences** What made Timbuktu a popular destination for Muslim scholars?

Songhai

6. **Compare and Contrast** How was the reign of Askia Muhammad similar to that of Mansa Musa?

Small Societies and Kingdoms of West Africa

7. **Analyze the Interaction** between Ife and Benin. How did this relationship benefit Benin?

8. **Cite Evidence** What factors led to the rise of prosperous trading kingdoms among the Hausa?

Lesson 7 Trading States of East Africa

CLOSE READING

Axum

1. **Determine Central Ideas** Explain how Axum profited from its location.

2. **Analyze Interactions** Explain how religious interactions influenced Axum's development.

Ethiopia

3. **Identify Cause and Effect** Explain how Christianity influenced Ethiopia's development.

4. **Analyze Interactions** How did Ethiopian Christianity reflect East African culture?

City-States of East Africa

5. **Analyze Interactions** What physical and geological features allowed trade to flourish in East Africa?

6. **Draw Inferences** Why would East African architecture have elements of Arabic design?

Great Zimbabwe

7. **Identify Cause and Effect** How did the Bantu migration influence the development of Great Zimbabwe?

European Exploration of Africa

8. **Determine Central Ideas** What spurred Portuguese traders to establish trading posts along the African coasts?

Lesson 8 Diverse Peoples and Traditions in Africa

CLOSE READING

Many Cultures and Patterns of Life

1. **Draw Conclusions** Why did family patterns vary greatly in medieval Africa?

2. **Analyze Interactions** Explain how a patrilineal family pattern worked.

3. **Identify Central Ideas** How did age play a role for children in some medieval African societies?

Government and Power

4. **Summarize** How does a power-sharing government in Africa work?

5. **Draw Inferences** Why might the opinions of older individuals carry more weight than the opinions of younger people?

Religion

6. **Determine Central Ideas** Why were Christianity and Islam able to absorb some of the beliefs of many African religions?

Art and Literature

7. **Identify Cause and Effect** Explain how art strengthened bonds within African communities.

8. **Summarize** Why were griots important to African society?

PRIMARY SOURCE EXPLORATION

Changing Approaches to Africa's History

Introduction

Ancient Egyptian, Greek, and Roman records offer historians early information about North and Northeast Africa. Our earliest written records of other parts of Africa, though, come from North Africans writing in Arabic. These travelers and historians were amazed and impressed by the wealth and power of West Africa's great kingdoms, such as the empire of Mali. During the nineteenth and early twentieth centuries, European nations colonized most of the continent of Africa. European writings of that time reflect Europeans' belief that Europe's culture and history were superior to Africa's culture and history. Some even believed that Africa had no real history. Since the 1950s, though, historians have gained respect for Africa's historical past and have worked to develop new approaches to uncovering it.

Document-Based Writing Activity

Analyze the following four sources and then use information from the documents and your knowledge of world history to write an essay in which you

- Describe how approaches to Africa's history have changed over time.
- Discuss the methods modern historians use to uncover the history of parts of Africa with limited written records.

Keep in mind that your essay should include an introduction, several paragraphs, and a conclusion. In the body of the essay, use evidence from at least three documents. Support your response with relevant facts, examples, and details. In developing your essay, be sure to keep these general definitions in mind:

- *Describe* means "to illustrate something in words or tell about it."
- *Discuss* means "to make observations about something using facts, reasoning, and argument; to present in some detail."

Source 1

History of the Berbers and the Muslim Dynasties of North Africa, part of the Book of Lessons, Ibn Khaldun, c. 1400

Ibn Khaldun, born in what is now Tunisia in 1332, has been called the father of modern history for his careful, critical, and factual approach to historical sources. His *Book of Lessons* is a history of the Muslim world, and it includes this glowing description of the West African empire of Mali, based on accounts from Arabic-speaking travelers and scholars who visited the kingdom or interacted with its rulers.

[T]he population of Mali increased so much that they took control of that whole region and subjugated the [people] of the neighboring countries. Having defeated the Sousou, they occupied all the states of that ancient kingdom and extended their control across the kingdom of Ghana to the Atlantic . . . They professed Islam, and it is said that the first of them to embrace that religion was a king called Bermendana. . . . Bermendana made the pilgrimage to Mecca, and the kings who followed him imitated his example. The most powerful of these monarchs was the one who subdued the Sousou . . . His name was Mari Djata [later known as Sundiata]. . . . His son Mansa Weli succeeded him. *Mansa*, in their language, means sultan. . . Authority passed from the children of Mari Djata to one of his sister's sons, named Abu-Bakr.

Mansa Musa, son and successor of Abu-Bakr, stood out as a ruler because of his power and the holiness of his life. Such was the justice of his administration that the memory of it is still alive. He made the pilgrimage [to Mecca] in the year A.H. 724 (A.D. 1324). . .

El-Mamer, whose truthfulness was well known, told me the following account of [his journey]: ". . . [W]e were part of the royal procession and were ahead of even the viziers and the leaders of the nation. His Majesty listened with pleasure to the stories that we told him, and, at each place where we stopped, he gave us a few dishes of food and sweets. Twelve thousand young enslaved men, dressed in brocade and Yemen silk tunics, carried his belongings."

Hajj Yunus, interpreter of [Mali] in Cairo, recounts the following: "King Mansa Musa arrived from his country with eighty loads of gold dust, each weighing three quintals [almost 300 pounds, or 135 kilograms] . . . "

1. How does Ibn Khaldun express his admiration for Mali?

2. What does his account suggest about the economy and society of Mali?

3. What can we tell about Ibn Khaldun's methods for researching and writing history?

Source 2

"African Historiography and the Challenges of European Periodization: A Historical Comment," Ihediwa Nkemjika Chimee, TRAFO–Blog for Transregional Research, July 31, 2018

Nigerian historian Ihediwa Nkemjika Chimee describes the dismissive attitude of European scholars toward African history during the colonial period. Africa's lack of written records posed a challenge to African historians seeking to recover the continent's history. Chimee explains how African historians used oral history and other sources to reconstruct Africa's past.

Some European authors . . . assailed and even doubted Africa's historical heritage; [English historian Hugh Trevor-Roper] even went as far as to say, "Africa had no history prior to European exploration and colonization, . . . there is only the history of Europeans in Africa. The rest is darkness", her past "the unedifying gyrations of barbarous tribes in picturesque but irrelevant corners of the globe." Even [German philosopher Georg Wilhelm Friedrich] Hegel, in an apparent attempt to besmirch Africa, once asserted that "Africa is no historical part of the world; it has no movement or development to exhibit." . . . These trenchant remarks about Africa's past all arose as a result of the inclination of a section of humanity to debase and denigrate another. The absence of written records in much of Africa posed a great challenge to the historical reconstruction of her past, and this was what spurred African scholars to evolve and insist on the use of oral history in reconstructing it, not minding the gaps inherent in this medium.

[Nigerian historian] Kenneth Dike [dee kay] was on hand to direct the emerging struggle to recover and reshape the soul of Africa's historical scholarship, among other peers in West Africa and other parts of black Africa. . . .Dike believed that subjecting oral history to systematic criticism and supplementing the resulting residue with evidence from written documents after the fashion of Western historiography, as well as with evidence derived from archaeology and other ancillary historical sciences, would put old-style African history through a process of rebirth.

Dike's efforts as a pioneer in African history later yielded the desired dividend with the emergence of many Africanist historians . . . The [African] authors of [the *UNESCO General History of Africa*] largely used oral evidence, archaeology and cultural and linguistic evidence to support their positions and arguments, thereby strengthening the new theory in African historical scholarship as championed by Dike.

1. According to Chimee, why did European scholars doubt the value of Africa's history?

2. How did African historians respond to the devaluing of their history?

3. How did African historians seek to avoid bias and safeguard objectivity when drawing on oral history?

Source 3

"The Empire of Mali," in Oxford Research Encyclopedia of African History, Sirio Canós-Donnay, 2019

In recent years, historians from other parts of the world, including Europe, have taken an interest in African history. Here, Spanish historian Sirio Canós-Donnay turns her attention to the empire of Mali, just as Ibn Khaldun did centuries ago. She uses some of the methods pioneered by modern African historians.

The Mali Empire is one of the largest and most widely known precolonial African states. It has featured in films, video games, works of fiction, and its memory is still a profound force in the articulation of social and political identities across [ethnically] Mande West Africa. Founded in the 13th century in the south of modern Mali, it quickly grew from a small kingdom to a vast empire stretching from the Senegambia in the west to Ivory Coast in the south. . . . In the absence of [local] written histories, knowledge of the Mali Empire has been based on a complex combination of oral traditions, medieval Arabic chronicles, European accounts, oral histories, and archaeology. Through a critical analysis of these sources, it has been possible to learn much about Mali's history, including aspects of its social organization, political structure, belief systems, and historical evolution. . . .

Both oral traditions and references in medieval Arabic accounts suggest the demise of Ghana/Wagadu in the late 11th century was followed by a period of political fragmentation in which a constellation of competing [states] strove for regional control. Two among them, the kingdoms of Sosso [or Sousou] and Mali, would eventually come to dominate the political landscape, and war between them ensued. The main source on this conflict is the [Sundiata] epic. Set in the 13th century, it narrates the life of the [Mande] prince [Sundiata] Keita and his exploits leading to the foundation of the Mali Empire. The epic begins with [Sundiata's] ancestry and describes how, after a troubled childhood and a prolonged exile, [Sundiata] returned to his homeland to unite all the Mande clans against the powerful Sumanguru Kante, king of Sosso. A long war followed until Sumanguru's final defeat at the battle of Krina. Following this victory, [Sundiata] reputedly set up the legal, political, and ideological framework of Mali's imperial structure. In some versions of the epic this framework was then consolidated in a "charter of rights" . . . but upon scrutiny this appears to have been a relatively modern addition, absent in earlier performances.

1. How does Canós-Donnay's account of Mali compare with Ibn Khaldun's?

2. How has Canós-Donnay been influenced by the methods presented in the previous source by Chimee?

3. Based on Canós-Donnay's account, how have the perspectives of European historians changed since the colonial period?

Source 4

The Horse in West African History: The Role of the Horse in the Societies of Pre-Colonial West Africa, Robin Law, republished 2020

This is the book cover for a recently published work on African history. The book is dedicated to West African history before European powers colonized this region.

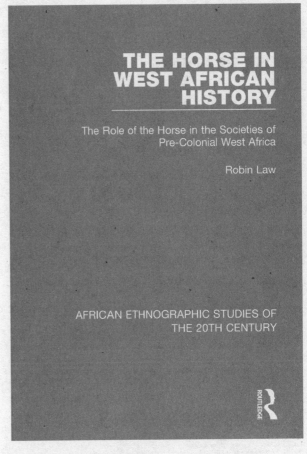

THE HORSE IN WEST AFRICAN HISTORY

The Role of the Horse in the Societies of Pre-Colonial West Africa

Robin Law

AFRICAN ETHNOGRAPHIC STUDIES OF THE 20TH CENTURY

ROUTLEDGE

1. What does the book's cover suggest about the nature of the book?

2. Based on the titles and labeling on the cover, what can you learn about this book?

3. What does this suggest about the book's subject matter?

Lesson 1 The Delhi Sultanate and Mughal India

CLOSE READING

The Delhi Sultanate

1. **Summarize** Identify one important reason why Muslim invaders were able to conquer much of India.

2. **Identify Cause and Effect** What effect did Tamerlane's invasion have on the Delhi Sultanate and India?

The Meeting of Islam and Hinduism

3. **Describe** Buddhism began in India. What was the effect of Muslim rule on Buddhism? Why?

4. **Infer** What can you infer from the fact that Urdu, a new language that combined elements of the Persian, Arabic, and Indian languages, was developed during the height of the Delhi Sultanate?

Sikhism Emerges

5. **Identify Supporting Details** Use the graphic organizer below to record details about Sikhism, such as its founder, key beliefs, and important practices.

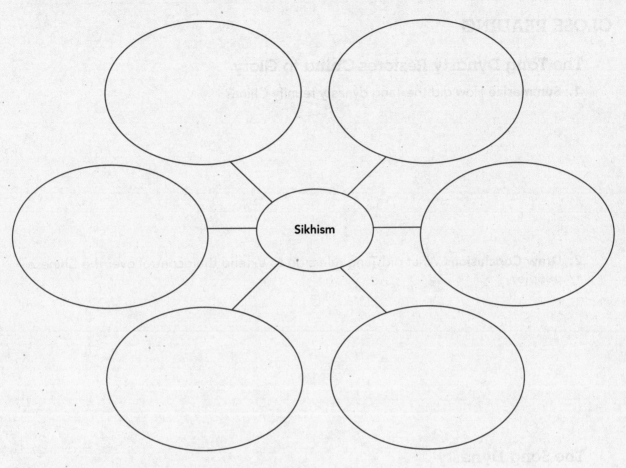

Sikhism

6. **Describe** What are the origins of Sikhism in India?

Mughal India

7. **Compare and Contrast** What are some key differences between Akbar's policies and those of his great-grandson, Aurangzeb?

8. **Identify Cause and Effect** What factors led to the fall of the Mughal empire in India?

Lesson 2 Golden Ages in China: Tang and Song Dynasties

CLOSE READING

The Tang Dynasty Restores China to Glory

1. **Summarize** How did the Tang dynasty reunify China?

2. **Draw Conclusions** What did Tang rulers do to extend their control over the Chinese people?

The Song Dynasty

3. **Identify Cause and Effect** How did the ability to grow two crops of rice each season instead of just one affect the Song economy and society?

4. **Analyze Visuals** What would make the invention of movable type block printing appealing to people outside of China?

An Ordered Society

5. Identify Supporting Details List one detail about each group in Tang and Song society.

Bureaucracy	Gentry	Peasants	Merchants

6. Draw Conclusions Why did members of the gentry have the leisure time to study the Confucian classics?

The Rich Culture of Tang and Song China

7. Summarize What were the major focuses of Chinese painting during this period?

8. Explain How did religious ideas influence the art of the Tang and Song dynasties?

Lesson 3 The Mongol Empire and Ming China

CLOSE READING

Mongols Build an Empire

1. **Sequence Events** Fill in the timeline below to record important events as you read this lesson.

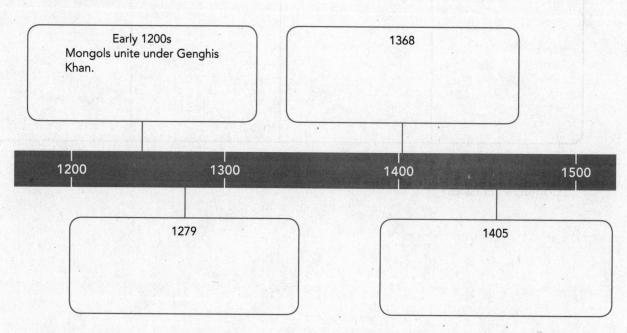

Early 1200s
Mongols unite under Genghis Khan.

1368

1200   1300   1400   1500

1279

1405

2. **Draw Inferences** Why did the Mongol armies find attacking China's walled cities difficult?

Mongols Rule China

3. **Identify Supporting Details** What details about Kublai Khan's actions reflect "an uneasy mix of Chinese and foreign customs"?

4. **Analyze Interactions** How do you think the visit of Marco Polo with Kublai Khan shows the impact Mongol rule had on China? Provide details from the text to support your discussion.

Chinese Rule Restored by the Ming

5. Identify Cause and Effect What major causes led to the founding of the Ming dynasty?

6. Cite Evidence How did agriculture improve during the Ming Dynasty, allowing the country to feed its enormous population? Cite evidence from the text to support your answer.

Chinese Fleets Explore the Seas

7. Draw Inferences Why do you think early Ming rulers sent Chinese fleets to distant regions? Cite evidence from the text and then discuss possible underlying reasons.

8. Identify Cause and Effect How did Zheng He's expeditions impact global trade? Use details from the text to support your answer.

Lesson 4 Korea and Its Traditions

CLOSE READING

The Geography of Korea

1. **Summarize** How did Korea's geography influence where people settled?

2. **Analyze Sequence** What aspect of Korea's location allowed it to be a cultural bridge?

The Silla and Koryo Dynasties Develop

3. **Analyze Interactions** What was the political relationship between China and different Korean dynasties during most of Korea's history?

4. **Determine Central Ideas** How was Chinese influence on Korea expanded during the Silla dynasty?

5. **Describe** Use the graphic organizer below to describe two important technological advances during the Koryo dynasty.

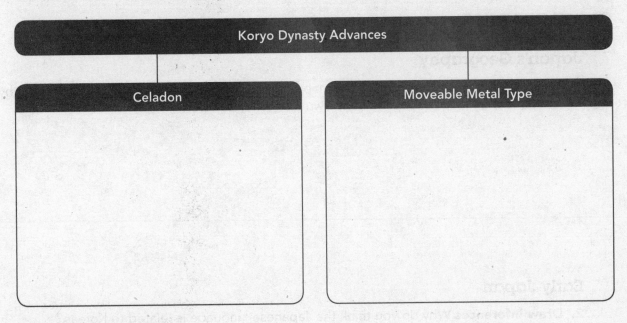

Koryo Dynasty Advances

Celadon	Moveable Metal Type

The Choson Dynasty

6. **Identify Cause and Effect** What important event led to the founding of the Choson dynasty?

7. **Compare and Contrast** What are some key differences between hangul and the Chinese system of writing?

8. **Draw Conclusions** What conclusion can you draw from the fact that, when they withdrew from Korea, the Japanese took with them many Korean artisans?

Lesson 5 The Island Kingdom of Japan

CLOSE READING

Japan's Geography

1. **Use Visual Information** Look at the map of early Japan and describe how the geography of the country helped it maintain its own distinctive culture.

Early Japan

2. **Draw Inferences** Why do you think the Japanese language is related to Korean?

Chinese Influence in Japan

3. **Draw Inferences** Why do you think Prince Shotoku sent students to study China directly rather than relying on Korean sources? Use details from the text to support your answer.

4. **Cite Evidence** Find evidence from the text that shows the Chinese influence in Japan.

Japanese Culture in the Heian Period

5. **Summarize** Describe life at the Heian court. What important role did women play?

Japan's Feudal Age

A United Japan

6. **Identify Supporting Details** As you read these two sections, use this chart to help you organize important details.

I. Japan's Feudal Age
   A.

II. A United Japan
   A.

Japanese Feudal Culture Evolves

7. **Compare and Contrast** Samurai in Japan practiced Zen Buddhism. What is surprising about this? Cite evidence from the text.

8. **Identify Supporting Details** How did Kabuki and bunraku shows mark a change in culture in Japan in the 1600s? Find evidence in the text to support your answer.

Lesson 6 The Many Cultures of Southeast Asia

CLOSE READING

The Geography of Southeast Asia

1. **Use Visual Information** Look at the map identifying the empires and kingdoms of Southeast Asia. Which parts of the region were likely more influenced by China? By India? Support your answer using details from the map.

2. **Draw Conclusions** Why was control of the Malacca and Sunda Straits important for any power that wanted to control trade with India and China? Cite evidence from the text and map to support your answer.

Indian Culture Spreads

3. **Determine Central Ideas** How did the monsoons influence the spread of Indian culture in Southeast Asia? Look for evidence in the text to support your answer.

4. **Summarize** What changes occurred in Southeast Asia as Indian culture spread in the region?

Kingdoms and Empires

5. **Compare and Contrast** Compare and contrast the Pagan Kingdom, the Khmer Empire, and the Srivijaya Empire. Using this table, identify where each began, which religions were most common, and one detail about each culture.

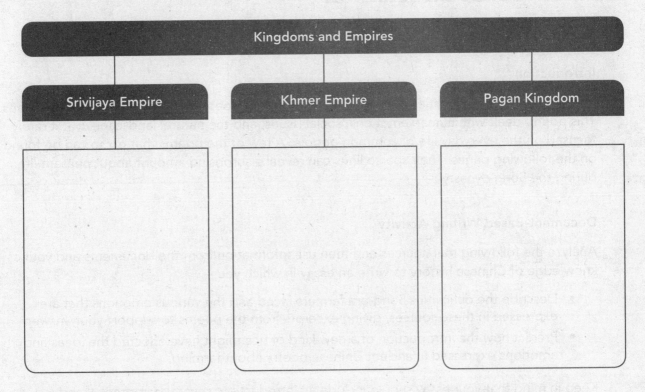

6. **Make Predictions** How might Srivijaya's location have made it differ from the Pagan Kingdom and the Khmer Empire?

The Rise of Vietnam

7. **Compare and Contrast** How was Vietnam's culture different from the cultures of other areas of Southeast Asia? What accounts for this difference?

8. **Sequence Events** How did Vietnam's relationship with China change from ancient times through A.D. 939?

PRIMARY SOURCE EXPLORATION

A Farmer's Life

Introduction

The Tang and Song dynasties are known for the brilliant poetry that flowed from writers' pens. This poetry dealt with human emotions, social issues, and the natural landscape, but it rarely focused on the everyday life of common people. A few of the poems that do so can be found on the following pages. Their sparse lines can reveal a surprising amount about peasant life during the Song dynasty.

Document-Based Writing Activity

Analyze the following four sources and then use information from the documents and your knowledge of Chinese history to write an essay in which you

- Describe the difficulties Song-era farmers faced and the various emotions that are expressed in these sources, giving excerpts from the poems to support your answer.
- Predict how the introduction of a new kind of rice might have affected the ideas and emotions expressed in ancient Chinese poetry about farming.

Keep in mind that your essay should include an introduction, several paragraphs, and a conclusion. In the body of the essay, use evidence from at least three documents. Support your response with relevant facts, examples, and details. In developing your essay, be sure to keep these general definitions in mind:

- *Describe* means "to illustrate something in words or tell about it."
- *Predict* means "to tell what will happen on the basis of observation, experience, or scientific reason."

Source 1

Excerpt from Random and Impromptu Seasonal Poems on Fields and Gardens, *Fan Chengda, 1200s*

While they were often poor, farmers were respected in ancient China because they fed a growing population. This excerpt describes a routine year for a farm family.

> On a lucky day we open our bundles of rice shoots;
> Thunder rumbles in the southern hills, it rains all night.
> This year no dearth of water for the seedling-beds:
> Look! Waves, newly risen, are lapping against the little bridge!
>
> Fifth month in Jian-Wu: the barleycorns are frigid;
> While planting seedlings we wear cotton coats over light jackets.
> Near paddy roots the tadpoles swim in clusters;
> Water in the fields this year is a foot deep.
>
> The newly made threshing yard is smooth as a mirror;
> Each family pounds rice while frosty, fair weather lasts.
> Amid the laughing and singing, a stirring of light thunder:
> Flails thrash throughout the night, echoing till dawn.
>
> Levy boats brimming with rice wait for granaries to open;
> Each single grain is like a pearl and white as frost.
> Don't grudge that two bushels carry a bushel in tax:
> Enough husks still remain to feed the boys full.

1. Look at the third line of the first stanza of the poem. What do the words "This year" tell you?

2. In the first line of the poem, why do you think the author considers it a "lucky day"?

3. What point is the poet making in the last two lines of the poem?

Source 2

"Feeling Sad for the Farmers," Yang Wanli, 1100s

Most farmers in Song China farmed small plots of land that they owned or rented from wealthier landowners. Life was difficult for these families. In addition to the back-breaking labor required to run a successful farm, farm families faced many other hardships.

the rice field looks like a rack of clouds
but there wasn't enough rain really

the field has turned yellow in the drought
and the yellowed ears have not matured

an early frost nipped the buckwheat
so the farmers will have to suffer

but there are thirteen lunar months this year
and they will suffer longer and how can they

This image shows farmers storing large quantities of rice at a granary.

1. What difficulties do the farmers in this poem face?

2. The traditional Chinese calendar is based on the moon and the sun. Some years have 12 and others have 13 lunar months. *Lunar* means "of, relating to, or resembling the moon." Based on this information, what is the poet saying in the last stanza?

3. Is the author of this poem likely a farmer? How do you know?

Source 3

Poems, Shu Yuexiang, 1200s

Women farmers were busy from sunup to sundown doing farm work, and they had cooking, cleaning, sewing, and other household chores to do as well. The excerpts below are from the poet Shu Yuexiang, who wrote during the 1200s.

> By the front hill the woman picking tea
> Quickly takes up her basket, revealing her take.
> The work is hard but she knows her task
> And sings and laughs without sign of sadness.
> Her eyebrows, reflected in the water, she doesn't paint.
> A flower is stuck in her hair, but she doesn't blush.
> Everyone cares about appearance,
> So why doesn't she comb her hair?
>
> At the edge of the field the waterwheel woman
> Draws the water to let it circulate.
> Her black hat is pushed to the side in the burning sun.
> Her blue skirt flaps noisily in the evening breeze.
> Over and over she repeats the same steps,
> Treading away on what seems to be empty space.
> I catch the sense of her work song:
> As long as you live, don't marry into a peasant family.

1. What does the poet mean when he writes "A flower is stuck in her hair, but she doesn't blush"?

2. Why does the poet conclude that the second woman is thinking "don't marry into a peasant family"? Refer to specific parts of the poem in your answer.

3. Compare this poem to Sources 1 and 2. Do they express similar or different ideas? Explain.

Source 4

Champa Rice Graphs

During the Song Dynasty, China had the world's largest population, with more than 100 million people. Feeding them required massive amounts of crops, which led to a search for ways to expand China's food supply. Drought-resistant Champa rice from Vietnam came to China around 1000 and quickly spread. Eventually, about 80% of the rice grown in some provinces was Champa rice.

Feeding China's Expanding Population

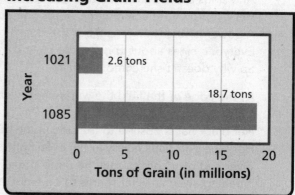

Sources: Data from Vaclav Smil, *China's Environmental Crisis*; Dieter Kuhn, *The Age of Confucian Rule: The Song Transformation of China*

Champa rice had a short growing season, allowing for two harvests a year instead of just one.

1. What happened to the population after Champa rice was introduced to China?

2. By how much did grain yields increase due to the introduction of Champa rice?

3. What does the fact that China obtained rice seeds from Vietnam tell you?

Lesson 1 The Italian Renaissance

CLOSE READING

The Italian Renaissance

1. Cite Evidence Which characteristics of the Italian Renaissance are present in modern-day American society and culture? Explain the Renaissance characteristics you think are present today with at least one example for each characteristic listed.

2. Draw Conclusions Explain how the work of Petrarch had an intellectual impact on generations in Europe after the Renaissance.

The Renaissance Begins in Italy

3. Identify Supporting Details What are some examples of how the great wealth and influence of the Medicis helped transform Florence into a prominent Renaissance city?

4. Integrate Information From Diverse Sources Use "Italy's City-States and Sea Trade" and the text to answer this question. What role did Italy's geography play in the development of the Renaissance?

Art Flourishes in the Renaissance

5. **Categorize** Fill in the chart below, which lists famous Renaissance artists and architects. In the right side of the chart, write the artist's accomplishments, such as a major work of art, a fresh approach, or a technical innovation that influenced later generations.

Renaissance Architects and Artists	Accomplishments
Leon Alberti	
Filippo Brunelleschi	
Leonardo da Vinci	
Michelangelo	
Raphael	

6. **Determine Meaning of Words** Read the last paragraph of "Leonardo da Vinci." What do you think the word *testament means* in the context of the last sentence? How was Leonardo's sketch book a testament to his genius? Use evidence from the text to support your answer.

New Books Reflect Renaissance Themes

7. **Draw Inferences** What characteristics of ruling families in Italian city-states during the Renaissance would Machiavelli, author of *The Prince*, have appreciated?

8. **Compare and Contrast** Compare and contrast the topics and themes that Machiavelli and Castiglione wrote about.

Lesson 2 The Renaissance in Northern Europe

CLOSE READING

Artists of the Northern Renaissance

1. **Summarize** What were some characteristics of northern European Renaissance paintings?

2. **Infer** In what ways did Albrecht Dürer's engravings reflect his own time period and culture, including his travels?

Northern European Humanists and Writers

3. **Identify Point of View** How did Erasmus's training as a priest sharpen his criticism of the Church? Give some examples from the text.

4. **Identify Effects** What were some long-term impacts of Shakespeare's writings?

5. **Draw Conclusions.** Complete the chart below to show some universal themes that writers such as Sir Thomas More, Rabelais, and Shakespeare addressed in their writings.

Humanist Author	Universal Theme Addressed
Sir Thomas More	
François Rabelais	
William Shakespeare	

The Printing Revolution

6. **Cite Evidence** The text states that the printing revolution "brought immense changes" to Northern Europe. Do you find this to be true or not? What evidence would you cite to support or debate this statement?

Lesson 3 The Protestant Reformation

CLOSE READING

Causes of the Reformation

1. **Summarize** What factors encouraged the Protestant Reformation?

2. **Draw Conclusions** Do you think the Protestant Reformation would have taken place if the printing press had not existed? Explain.

Martin Luther's Protests Bring Change

3. **Summarize** Why did Luther gain an immediate following?

4. **Determine Central Ideas** What ideas did Luther share with humanist scholars?

5. **Analyze Sequence** Describe the sequence of events that led to Martin Luther successfully founding Lutheranism. Fill in each step in the chart below.

	Steps Towards Establishing Lutheranism
1.	Luther posts the 95 Theses, outlining church abuses, to a church door in Wittenberg.
2.	
3.	
4.	
5.	
6.	

John Calvin Challenges the Church

6. **Draw Conclusions** What aspects of Calvinism might have appealed to people in a time of uncertainty?

7. **Contrast** What is the key difference between Lutheranism and Calvinism regarding salvation?

8. **Determine Central Ideas** Why did Calvin and other church leaders choose to set up a theocracy in Geneva?

Lesson 4 Reformation Ideas Spread

CLOSE READING

An Explosion of Protestant Sects

1. **Identify Cause and Effect** Why did Protestants develop many different sects, rather than all embracing Lutheranism?

The English Reformation

2. **Draw Inferences** Why was the pope's denial of Henry VIII's request for an annulment so critical to the formation of the Church of England?

3. **Identify Supporting Details** What is significant about the fact that during the dissolution of the monasteries, Henry "granted some church lands to nobles and other high-ranking citizens"?

4. **Draw Conclusions** How might Mary's burning of heretics have strengthened the Protestant cause in England?

5. **Summarize** How did the Elizabethan Settlement affect the Reformation in England?

The Catholic Reformation

6. **Summarize** What were the basic components of the Catholic Reformation? Use evidence from the text to support your statements.

7. **Draw Inference** What does the term *Counter-Reformation* imply about the causes of this movement?

8. **Cite Evidence** Read the text under "Results of the Catholic Reformation" and cite evidence that the Catholic Reformation achieved its basic goals.

Religious Persecution Continues

9. **Summarize** Why was religious persecution widespread during the Reformation?

Lesson 5 The Scientific Revolution

CLOSE READING

Changing Views of the Universe

1. **Identify Cause and Effect** Why would the social, political, and intellectual changes of the Renaissance encourage changes in science?

2. **Identify Central Issues** Why did many scientists and the Church reject Copernicus's hypothesis that the universe was heliocentric?

3. **Draw Conclusions** How might the Reformation have shaped the Church's response to Galileo's discoveries?

A New Scientific Method

4. **Summarize** What were the contributions of the philosophers Francis Bacon and René Descartes to science?

5. Identify Steps in a Process Identify the steps in the scientific method.

Breakthroughs in Medicine and Chemistry

6. Summarize What are some of the medical advances made during the 1500s and 1600s?

7. Draw Conclusions In what ways did the scientific method differ from earlier approaches to learning?

8. Identify Cause and Effect What impact did Renaissance ideas have on medicine during the Scientific Revolution?

9. Synthesize How did Newton use mathematics in his work?

PRIMARY SOURCE EXPLORATION

The Life of an Artist in Renaissance Italy

Introduction

In Renaissance Italy, art was serious business. Painters and sculptors were required to study under masters of their craft. They had to learn both classical styles and new techniques. Once they were ready to strike out on their own, they had to attract patronage – whether from the Church, a city government, or a wealthy aristocrat. In the end, the hard work paid off and produced some of the greatest works of art in history.

Document-Based Writing Activity

Analyze the following four sources and then use information from the documents and your knowledge of world history to write an essay in which you

- Describe the knowledge and skills Renaissance artists had to master.
- Evaluate the role of patronage in the Italian Renaissance.

Keep in mind that your essay should include an introduction, several paragraphs, and a conclusion. In the body of the essay, use evidence from at least three documents. Support your response with relevant facts, examples, and details. In developing your essay, be sure to keep these general definitions in mind:

- *Describe* means "to illustrate something in words or tell about it."
- *Evaluate* means "to examine and judge the significance, worth, or condition of; to determine the value of."

Source 1

The Craftman's Handbook, Cennino Cennini

Cennino Cennini was an early Renaissance painter. He learned his craft from his father, who in turn studied under the great medieval painter Giotto. Around 1400, Cennini wrote *The Craftman's Handbook*, a book of instructions for young apprentices working in artists' shops. In it, he covers such duties as mixing pigments, caring for brushes, and painting on wood, plaster, or canvas.

Know that there ought not to be less time spent in learning than this: to begin as a shopboy studying for one year, to get practice in drawing on the little panel; next to serve in a shop under some master to learn how to work at all the branches which pertain to our profession; and to stay and begin the working up of colors; and to learn to boil the sizes [material used to prepare paper or cloth], and grind the gessos [chalks]; and to get experience in gessoing anconas [moldings], and modeling and scraping them; gilding and stamping; for the space of a good six years. Then to get experience in painting, embellishing with [dyes], making cloths of gold, getting practice in working on the wall, for six more years; drawing all the time, never leaving off, either on holidays or on workdays. And in this way your talent, through much practice, will develop into real ability. Otherwise, if you follow other systems, you need never hope that they will reach any high degree of perfection. For there are many who say that they have mastered the profession without having served under masters. Do not believe it, for I give you the example of this book: even if you study it by day and by night, if you do not see some practice under some master you will never amount to anything, nor will you ever be able to hold your head up in the company of masters.

1. What is the minimum amount of time Cennini thinks a young painter should spend working and studying under a master?

2. How does the apprenticeship benefit both the apprentice and the master?

3. According to Cennini, what is the difference between talent and ability? What role does education play?

Source 2

Raphael, The Marriage of the Virgin, 1504

Renaissance painters had to learn all the techniques perfected by classical and medieval artists. In addition, they had to master new techniques, especially perspective. These images demonstrate how perspective worked in *The Marriage of the Virgin* by the Italian Renaissance master Raphael.

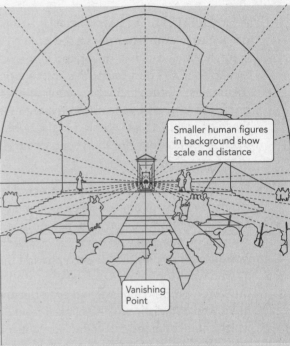

Smaller human figures in background show scale and distance

Vanishing Point

Like many Renaissance paintings, *The Marriage of the Virgin* depicted a Biblical subject—the wedding of Joseph to Mary, the mother of Jesus—in a contemporary Italian setting. The schematic at the right shows how Raphael used perspective to create a sense of depth.

1. Based on these images, how does the vanishing point work in painting?

2. How does the sizing of figures create a sense of depth? How does this mirror how your vision works in real life?

3. What branches of knowledge did Renaissance painters have to understand in order to develop the rules of perspective?

Source 3

Lorenzo de Medici, from Lives of the Artists, *Giorgio Vasari, 1550*

At the height of the Italian Renaissance, wealthy patrons often did more than commission works of art. Some also played a major role in the education of young artists. Here, painter and author Giorgio Vasari describes how Lorenzo de Medici of Florence took sculptor Pietro Torrigiano under his patronage.

In his youth [Torrigiano] was taken by Lorenzo de' Medici the elder (Il Magnifico) into the garden which the latter possessed on the Piazza of San Marco in Florence, and which that magnificent citizen had decorated in the richest manner with figures from the antique and examples of the best sculptures. In the loggie, the walks, and all the buildings there were the noblest statues in marble, admirable works of the ancients, with pictures and other productions of art by the most eminent masters, whether of Italy or of other countries. All these treasures, to say nothing of the noble ornament they formed to the garden, were as a school or academy for the young painters and sculptors, as well as for all others devoted to the arts of design. . . .

But men of genius were always protected by the magnificent Lorenzo, and more especially did he favour such of the nobles as he perceived to have an inclination for the study of art; and it is therefore no matter of astonishment that masters should have proceeded from this school, some of whom have awakened the surprise, as well as the admiration, of the world. And not only did Lorenzo provide the means of instruction, but also those of life for all who were too poor to pursue their studies without such aid; nay, he further supplied them with proper clothing, and even bestowed considerable presents on any one among them who had distinguished himself from his fellows by some well-executed design; all which so encouraged the young students of our arts that, laboring in emulation of each other, many of them became excellent masters.

1. How does this description suggest the Renaissance appreciation of the classical art of Greece and Rome?

2. What services did Lorenzo offer to aspiring artists?

3. Why do you think Lorenzo chose to spend part of his fortune in this manner?

Source 4

Letter From Michelangelo to Giovanni di Pistoia, 1509

As a youth in Florence, Michelangelo enjoyed the patronage of Lorenzo de Medici. Years later, he was commissioned by the Pope to paint the ceiling of the Sistine Chapel. In this poem, Michelangelo – who considered himself primarily a sculptor – describes the task.

I've already grown a goiter from this torture,
hunched up here like a cat in Lombardy
(or anywhere else where the stagnant water's poison).
My stomach's squashed under my chin, my beard's
pointing at heaven, my brain's crushed in a casket,
my [torso] twists like a harpy's. My brush,
above me all the time, dribbles paint
so my face makes a fine floor for droppings!

My haunches are grinding into my guts....
Every gesture I make is blind and aimless.
My skin hangs loose below me, my spine's
all knotted from folding over itself.
I'm bent taut as a Syrian bow.

Because I'm stuck like this, my thoughts
are crazy, perfidious tripe:
anyone shoots badly through a crooked blowpipe.

My painting is dead.
Defend it for me, Giovanni, protect my honor.
I am not in the right place—I am not a painter.

---

1. Describe two physical discomforts Michelangelo endured while painting the Sistine Chapel.

2. How do you think Michelangelo felt about the Pope at this point?

3. What does this poem suggest about the relationship between artists and patrons?

Lesson 1 Europeans Explore Overseas

CLOSE READING

Causes of European Exploration

1. **Analyze Information** Why did Europeans find potentially dangerous sea routes preferable to overland routes?

Portugal Explores the Seas

2. **Cite Evidence** Why did Prince Henry think it was worthwhile for the Portuguese to explore the coast of Africa? Cite evidence from the text to support your answer.

3. **Summarize** How did the Portuguese use education and technology for their voyages of exploration?

Columbus Searches for a Route to Asia

4. **Compare and Contrast** How were Ferdinand and Isabella's reasons for sponsoring Columbus's voyages of exploration similar to or different from Prince Henry's reasons for sponsoring Portuguese exploration?

5. **Hypothesize** How do you think Native Americans would have responded to news about the Treaty of Tordesillas and the Line of Demarcation?

The Search for a Route to the Pacific

6. **Compare and Contrast** In the late 1400s and early 1500s, how was exploration of the Americas by the English, Dutch, and French similar to or different from exploration of the Americas by the Spanish?

European Expansion in Africa

7. **Integrate Information from Diverse Sources** Read the first two paragraphs of "The Dutch Settle Cape Town." Then look at the illustration showing a busy 1683 harbor scene at Cape Town. What do the text and the illustration convey about the Cape Town? What different information about the Dutch settlement can you draw from these two sources?

8. **Make Predictions** In the years after the French and British began to establish footholds in Africa, they would come into conflict with each other all around the world. Predict what you think will cause conflict between France and Britain.

Lesson 2 Europeans Gain Footholds in Asia

CLOSE READING

Portugal Builds an Empire in Asia

1. **Summarize** How did the Portuguese establish a strong trading position in Asia?

Rise of the Dutch and the Spanish

2. **Analyze Information** Why did the leaders of the Netherlands give so much power to the Dutch East India Company?

3. **Identify Central Issues** How did the location of the Philippines make it a valuable asset for Spain?

Europeans Trade in Mughal India

4. **Infer** The Mughal empire gave trading rights to several European countries. What does this suggest about the Mughal empire's assumptions about the power of those European countries?

Ming China and Europe

5. Analyze Interactions Why do you think the Ming eventually allowed the Portuguese and other Europeans to have some limited trade with Chinese merchants?

The Manchus Conquer China

6. Identify Cause and Effect What factors contributed to peace and prosperity in Qing China?

7. Draw Inferences What do Qing China's trade policies with European nations in the 1700s tell you about the state of the Qing economy?

Korea and Japan Choose Isolation

8. Compare Why did both Japan and Korea respond to increased foreign contact by adopting a policy of isolation?

Lesson 3 European Conquests in the Americas

CLOSE READING

First Encounters

1. **Sequence Events** As you read this lesson, keep track of the sequence of events that led to the establishment of a Spanish empire in the Americas by completing the chart below.

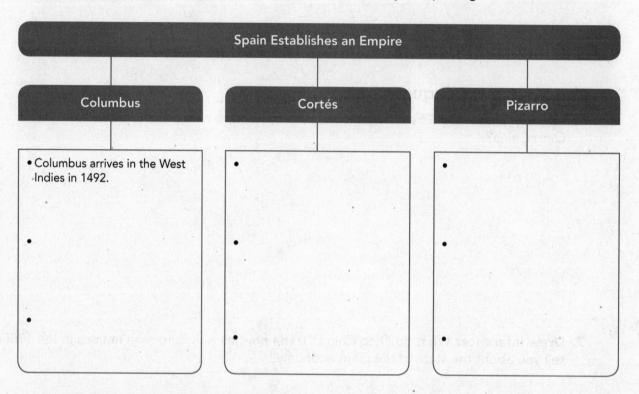

Spain Establishes an Empire

| Columbus | Cortés | Pizarro |

- Columbus arrives in the West Indies in 1492.
-
-

2. **Identify Supporting Details** What details under "The Taínos Meet Columbus" support the idea that the Spanish treated the Taínos harshly?

Cortés Conquers the Aztecs

3. **Cite Evidence** Why did many Native American groups agree to make alliances with Cortés? Cite evidence from the text in support of your answer.

The Incan Empire and Beyond

4. Infer How do you think the bloody civil war between Atahualpa and his brother may have affected the ability of the Incas to resist Pizarro?

Governing the Spanish Empire

5. Cite Evidence How did the Catholic Church work with the government to convert Native Americans to Christianity and to make them loyal Spanish subjects? Cite evidence from the text to support your answer.

6. Analyze Information How did the introduction of sugar cane to the Americas impact Native Americans and Africans? Support your answer with details from the text.

Society and Culture in Spanish America

7. Make Generalizations How did a person's occupation in Spanish colonial society reflect his or her social class? Supply details from the text to support your response.

The Impact of Spanish Colonization

8. Contrast How did the impact of Spanish colonization in the Americas differ for the Spanish and Native Americans? Cite evidence from the text to support your answer.

Lesson 4 European Colonies in North America

CLOSE READING

New France

1. **Identify Cause and Effect** How did the climate and physical features of Canada affect French colonization in the region?

2. **Summarize** How was the government of New France structured?

The 13 English Colonies

3. **Compare** How did the new English colonies at Jamestown and Plymouth survive?

4. **Draw Conclusions** Why did English colonists have more self-government than the colonists of New France? Use details from the text to elaborate.

5. **Compare and Contrast** In the table below, list three English colonial regions of North America. Then describe the kind of economy each colonial region had.

English Colonial Region	Economy

A Power Struggle Begins

6. **Describe** How did the Treaty of Paris in 1763 result in a redrawing of the map of North America for both Britain and France?

7. **Identify Main Ideas** How did the Seven Years' War affect the balance of power in North America?

Lesson 5 The Slave Trade and Its Impact on Africa

CLOSE READING

The Trade in Enslaved Africans Expands

1. **Determine Central Ideas** What is a main point about slavery that is communicated in the Slavery Throughout History section?

2. **Analyze Interactions** Read the section in this text called "African Resistance." How did some African leaders try to resist the trade in enslaved people? What were the European responses to these efforts?

The Atlantic Slave Trade

3. **Analyze Sequence** Read the text and look at the triangular trade map. Use the flowchart below to show the general sequence of events in the triangular trade (i.e., What were the first, second, and third legs of the triangular trade?).

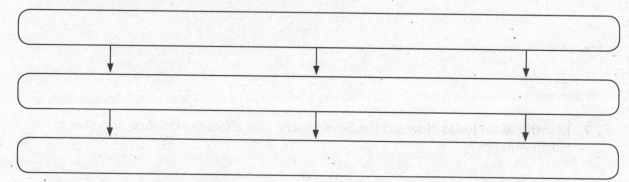

4. **Summarize** How did port cities in New England benefit from the trade in enslaved people even though few enslaved Africans were brought to work in New England?

Horrors of the Middle Passage

5. **Identify Supporting Details** The author makes the statement that "For enslaved Africans, the Middle Passage was a horror." Find and list some details from the text that support this statement.

6. **Determine Central Ideas** Why does the author use the phrase "floating coffins" to describe slave ships?

Impact of the Slave Trade

7. **Describe** How were the Americas affected by the trade in enslaved Africans?

8. **Integrate Information from Diverse Sources** Use the information from the chart "The Atlantic Slave Trade" and the text to describe the effect of slavery on Africans.

Lesson 6 Effects of Global Contact

CLOSE READING

The Columbian Exchange

1. **Identify Cause and Effect** As you read this text, fill in the flowchart to analyze the causes and effects of the Columbian Exchange.

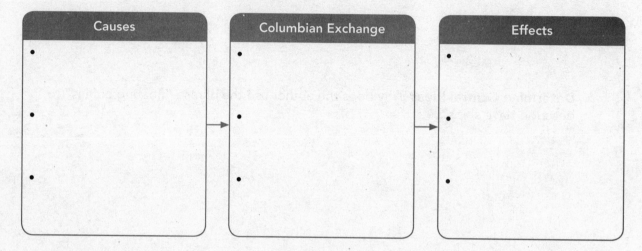

Causes	Columbian Exchange	Effects
•	•	•
•	•	•
•	•	•

2. **Compare and Contrast** Consider the Columbian Exchange and its effects on populations in Africa, Europe, and the Americas. How did the exchanges cause some populations to decline in number, while others rose in number?

A Commercial Revolution

3. **Identify Cause and Effect:** What were some effects of the growth of European capitalism?

4. **Draw Inferences** Read the section called "New Business Methods" What are some modern-day examples of joint-stock companies? Both in the past and today, what are the potential risks and rewards for investors?

Mercantilism

5. **Identify Steps in a Process** By what steps did European governments put mercantilist principles into practice?

6. **Assess an Argument** Consider the following statement: "The Commercial Revolution was very beneficial for European society." How valid is that statement? Cite evidence from the text that supports or does not support the statement.

PRIMARY SOURCE EXPLORATION

The Problem of Piracy

Introduction

Piracy is defined as any attack or robbery carried out by ships against another ship or a coastal town. Piracy has been around since at least the 1300s B.C., when sea raiders attacked merchants ships from ancient Egypt and other Mediterranean civilizations. In the 1500s, piracy had become common in the Caribbean, with many pirates – known as privateers – acting with the unofficial authority of their monarchs. The period from about 1650 to 1740 is known as the Golden Age of Piracy, when many of our modern romantic notions of piracy took shape. But for victims of piracy in the Caribbean, the Indian Ocean, the African coast, and elsewhere, there was nothing romantic about piracy at all.

Document-Based Writing Activity

Analyze the following four sources and then use information from the documents and your knowledge of world history to write an essay in which you

- Explain why governments approved some acts of piracy.
- Discuss the difference between romantic notions of piracy and the reality.

Keep in mind that your essay should include an introduction, several paragraphs, and a conclusion. In the body of the essay, use evidence from at least three documents. Support your response with relevant facts, examples, and details. In developing your essay, be sure to keep these general definitions in mind:

- *Explain* means "to make plain or understandable; to give reasons for or causes of; to show the logical development or relationships of."
- *Discuss* means "to make observations about something using facts, reasoning, and argument; to present in some detail."

Source 1

Image of Sir Francis Drake being knighted by Queen Elizabeth I

Privateer, explorer, admiral – Francis Drake was one of the most colorful figures in English history.

- In the 1570s, Drake led a series of raids against Spanish settlements in the Caribbean, including an attack on a Spanish mule train laden with 20 tons of gold and silver. The king of Spain reportedly offered a reward for his capture that would be worth millions today.

- From 1577–1580, Drake commanded the second voyage to circumnavigate the world. He was also the first commander to complete the voyage, since the Spanish explorer Magellan had been killed before reaching home.

- In 1588, Drake was second in command of the British fleet that defeated the Spanish Armada in its attempt to attack Britain.

Queen Elizabeth I granted Drake a knighthood in 1881. The image at right shows the queen knighting Drake aboard his ship, the *Golden Hind*.

Although images like this became popular in England, the knighthood ceremony was actually performed by a French diplomat whose support Elizabeth was seeking.

1. For which of his accomplishments do you think Elizabeth granted Drake a knighthood?

2. Why do you think Drake was considered a hero by the English despite his piracy?

3. How do you think the Spanish responded to Drake being knighted? Explain.

Source 2

Transcript of the Trial of Captain Kidd, 1701

In 1701, Scottish seaman William Kidd was found guilty of seizing an Armenian merchant ship in the Indian Ocean. At the time, Britain authorized its navy to seize ships sailing under French protection. Kidd was hanged for piracy and murder. Since then, historians have debated whether Kidd deserves his reputation as a pirate.

Piracy Charge

That William Kidd, late of London . . . did piratically and feloniously set upon, board, break, and enter a certain merchant ship, called the *Quedagh Merchant* . . . and carry away the said merchant ship, called the *Quedagh Merchant*, and the apparel and tackle of the same ship, of the value of £400 of lawful money of England; 70 chests of opium, of the value of £1400 of lawful money of England ; 250 bags of sugar, of the value of £100 of lawful money of England; 20 bales of raw silk, of the value of £400 of lawful money of England ; 100 bales of callicoes, of the value of £200 of lawful money of England. . . .

Kidd's Defense

Dr. Oldish—It is very true, he is charged with piracies in several ships; but they had French passes when the seizure was made. Now, if there were French passes, it was a lawful seizure. . . .

Mr. Lemmon—My lord, I desire one word as to this circumstance; he was doing his King and country service, instead of being a pirate. . . .

Murder Charge

The Solicitor-General— My lord, and gentlemen of the jury, we will prove this as particular as can be, that William Kidd was captain of the ship, and that William Moore was under him in the ship, and without any provocation he gave him this blow whereof he died.

Mr. Coniers—My lord, it will appear to be a most barbarous fact, to murder a man in this manner; for the man gave him no manner of provocation. This William Moore was a gunner in the ship, and this William Kidd abused him, and called him a "lousy dog ;" and upon a civil answer he took this bucket and knocked him on the head, whereof he died the next day.

---

1. How did Kidd's actions with regard to the *Quedagh Merchant* fit the definition of piracy?

2. Explain Kidd's defense in your own words. Do you agree with his defense?

3. What image of Kidd does the murder charge create?

Source 3

A General History of the Pyrates, "Captain Charles Johnson" (1724)

A *General History of the Robberies and Murders of the Most Notorious Pyrates* helped popularize many of our ideas about pirates. The actual identity of the author, "Captain Johnson" is unknown. In this excerpt, he describes how Edward Teach – the English pirate known as Blackbeard – blockaded the town of Charleston, South Carolina, in 1717.

They took here a Ship as she was coming out, bound for London, commanded by Robert Clark, with some Passengers on Board for England . . . all which being done in the Face of the Town, struck a great Terror to the whole Province of Carolina, having just before been visited by Vane, another notorious Pyrate, that they abandoned themselves to Dispair, being in no Condition to resist their Force. They were eight Sail in the Harbour, ready for the Sea, but none dared to venture out, it being almost impossible to escape their Hands. The inward bound Vessels were under the same unhappy Dilemma, so that the Trade of this Place was totally interrupted. . .

Teach detained all the Ships and Prisoners, and, being in want of Medicines, resolves to demand a Chest from the Government of the Province; accordingly Richards, the Captain of the Revenge Sloop, with two or three more Pyrates, were sent up along with Mr. Marks, one of the Prisoners, whom they had taken in Clark's Ship, and very insolently made their Demands, threatning, that if they did not send immediately the Chest of Medicines, and let the Pyrate-Ambassadors return, without offering any Violence to their Persons, they would murder all their Prisoners, send up their Heads to the Governor, and set the Ships they had taken on Fire. . . .

Captain Teach, assumed the Cognomen of Black-beard, from that large Quantity of Hair, which, like a frightful Meteor, covered his whole Face, and frightened America more than any Comet that has appeared there a long Time.

This Beard was black, which he suffered to grow of an extravagant Length; as to Breadth, it came up to his Eyes; he was accustomed to twist it with Ribbons, in small Tails. . . . In Time of Action, he wore a Sling over his Shoulders, with three brace of Pistols, hanging in Holsters like Bandaliers; and stuck lighted Matches under his Hat, which appearing on each Side of his Face, his Eyes naturally looking fierce and wild, made him altogether such a Figure, that Imagination cannot form an Idea of a Fury, from Hell, to look more frightful.

1. According to this account, what did Blackbeard want and how did he get it?

2. What was the psychological and economic impact of Blackbeard's attack on Charleston?

3. How does the author's description of Blackbeard's appearance compare with your own image of pirates? Do you think it is accurate?

Source 4

Modern-Day Somali Piracy

Piracy made news again in the early 2000s. Somali pirates attacked hundreds of vessels in the Arabian Sea and Indian Ocean and kidnaped more than 1,000 people. The first document is from a UN report. The second is by a journalist held hostage in Somalia.

Report of the Secretary-General of the United Nations, 2010

[I]n the first nine months of 2011 there were 185 attacks against ships in the waters off the coast of Somalia, resulting in the hijacking of 28 ships. . . .

This development has amplified the threat of piracy to all ships transiting the Indian Ocean, which has in turn increased insurance premiums paid by the maritime industry. Together with the ever higher ransoms paid, and time-consuming route changes, shipping costs are on the rise, with detrimental effects to the global economy.

Somali piracy has evolved into a sophisticated organized crime. Pirate gangs' increasing income from higher ransoms has strengthened their strike capability. In 2011, using better and heavier weapons, pirates have targeted more oil tankers and sailing vessels. Violence against seafarers has also increased. . . .

I am deeply concerned at the fate of the victims from all over the world who remain in the hands of the pirate criminals. Most often, they are kept in difficult and inhumane conditions.

"My 977 days held hostage by Somali pirates," Michael Scott Moore, 2015

We sped out of town to the east, and I sat with ripped clothes and a bleeding scalp, squeezed into the back seat next to three surly gunmen. . . .

Near sundown we arrived at an outdoor camp in a reddish, sandy part of the bush. The pirates blindfolded me and led me to a foam mattress, which lay in the open beside a crumbling low cliff. I was dazed and bloodied but aware of other Somali gunmen, and other hostages. I saw very little. Without my glasses I am drastically nearsighted, and I spent my entire captivity, more than two and a half years, in a fuzzy state of near-blindness.

The guards handed me bread, a bottle of water and a can of tuna. That would be my diet for the next several months, along with occasional cooked pasta or rice. In two months, I would lose about 40 pounds.

1. According to the UN report, what were the effects of Somali piracy?

2. How can you tell that Moore was subject to violence by the pirates?

3. How does Moore's account support statements made in the UN report?

Lesson 1 Absolute Monarchy in Spain and France

CLOSE READING

Ruling with Absolute Power

1. **Explain an Argument** If Louis XIV truly ruled by divine right, what risk did his subjects run if they questioned his authority?

Spain and the Hapsburg Empire

2. **Summarize** What role did religion play in the policies of Charles V?

Philip II Becomes an Absolute Monarch

3. **Draw Inferences** What decisions did Spanish rulers make that weakened Spain's economy?

Arts and Literature of Spain's Golden Century

4. **Draw Conclusions** What is one reason the arts might have flourished during this period of Spanish history?

Royal Power Expands in France

5. **Identify Cause and Effect** How did Richelieu's treatment of the nobles and the Huguenots strengthen the monarchy?

Louis XIV, an Absolute Monarch

6. **Determine Author's Point of View** Louis XIV called himself the "Sun King" and said, "I am the State." Describe how each statement reflects absolutism, and explain which you find to be the best "slogan" for Louis XIV.

The Royal Palace at Versailles

7. **Cite Evidence** How did Louis control the nobles? Use examples from the text.

The Legacy of Louis XIV

8. **Analyze Interactions** Why did Louis XIV expel the Huguenots? In your opinion, was it a good decision or a bad decision? Why?

Lesson 2 Rise of Austria, Prussia, and Russia

CLOSE READING

The Thirty Years' War

1. **Identify Cause and Effect** How did the Thirty Years' War affect the Holy Roman Empire?

Hapsburg Austria Expands

2. **Draw Inferences** What kinds of conflicts could emerge in an empire as diverse as the Hapsburg Empire?

Prussia Emerges

3. **Cite Evidence** How did Frederick William I gain the loyalty of the Prussian nobles? Can you think of two other methods that absolutist rulers have used to control their nobility? Which were most successful? Why?

4. **Paraphrase** What does the phrase "Prussia is not a state which possesses an army, but an army which possesses a state" mean? What does this say about Prussia's values?

Peter the Great Modernizes Russia

5. **Cite Evidence** How did Peter the Great westernize Russia? Cite at least three examples.

Expanding Russia's Borders

6. **Draw Inferences** What is one reason that Peter the Great greatly expanded the military during his reign?

Catherine the Great

7. **Compare and Contrast** How were Catherine the Great's goals similar to those of Peter? How did they differ?

8. **Categorize** Catherine the Great continued Peter the Great's efforts to westernize Russia and was also a ruthless leader like her predecessors. Give examples of both her reforms and her repression in a paragraph in which you assess Catherine's strength as a leader.

Five Great European Powers

9. **Determine Central Ideas** In the 1500s and 1600s, alliances between countries were formed based on religion. In the 1700s, what were these alliances based on? What does this say about trends within European politics?

Lesson 3 The Triumph of Parliament in England

CLOSE READING

Tudor Monarchs Work with Parliament

1. **Cite Evidence** How did Elizabeth I handle her relationship with Parliament? Why do you think this was the case? Cite evidence from the text in your answer.

Stuart Monarchs Clash with Parliament

2. **Analyze Interactions** Why did Parliament react so negatively to James I's speech about divine right?

The English Civil War

3. **Analyze Sequence** Use this graphic organizer to help you take notes about the sequence of events leading up to the English Civil War.

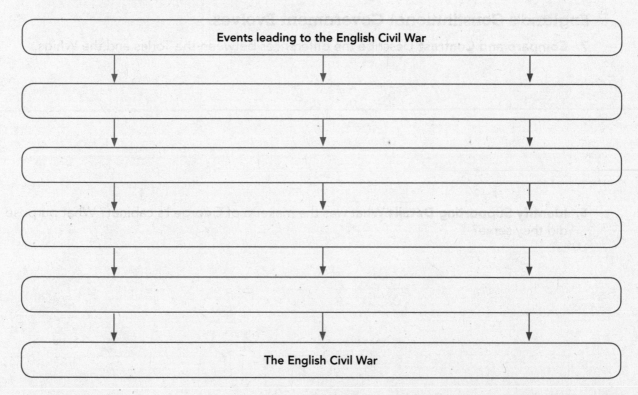

Events leading to the English Civil War

The English Civil War

4. **Identify Supporting Details** What are some reasons for the Roundhead victory?

Cromwell and the Commonwealth

5. **Summarize** What happened in Ireland during the Commonwealth period, and why?

From Restoration to Glorious Revolution

6. **Summarize** What was the English Bill of Rights? What was its impact?

England's Constitutional Government Evolves

7. **Compare and Contrast** Describe the differences between the Tories and the Whigs.

8. **Identify Supporting Details** What was the makeup of George I's cabinet? What purpose did they serve?

Lesson 4 The Enlightenment

CLOSE READING

Scientific Revolution Leads to the Enlightenment

1. **Determine Central Ideas** Advances in science convinced many educated Europeans of the power of human reason. How did an emphasis on human reason lead to developments in other areas of life?

Hobbes and Locke on the Role of Government

2. **Draw Conclusions** Thomas Hobbes argued that people entered into a social contract, an agreement by which they gave up their freedom for an organized society. Give two examples of how we must give up absolute freedom to live in an ordered society.

3. **Draw Conclusions** John Locke proposed that if a government fails in its obligations, the people have the right to overthrow their government. What are some of the obligations you believe a government owes to its people?

The *Philosophes*

4. **Analyze Interactions** Which of the Enlightenment thinkers described in this section had the greatest influence on the actual structure of the U.S. government? What was his contribution?

New Economic Ideas

5. Determine Central Ideas What are two differences between the physiocrats and the mercantilists?

Spread of Enlightenment Ideas

6. Identify Key Steps in a Process List three ways Enlightenment ideas spread during the 1700s.

Arts and Literature of the Enlightenment

7. Cite Evidence How did the middle class influence the arts, literature, and music of the period? Support your ideas with examples from the reading.

The Enlightened Despots

8. Draw Inferences Look back through the reading and find one reform that all three enlightened despots enacted. Why do you believe this reform was a universal theme among these absolute rulers?

Lesson 5 The American Revolution

CLOSE READING

Britain Becomes a Global Power

1. **Analyze Interactions** If you were a member of the British Parliament in the 1760s, would you have supported George III's attempt to consolidate power? Explain your answer.

The British Colonies in America

2. **Vocabulary: Determine Meaning** Reread the paragraph that discusses the Navigation Acts. Using the context of the paragraph, what does the term *mercantilist* mean?

Discontent in the Colonies

3. **Determine Central Ideas** Why do you think that the Enlightenment ideals of liberty and equality had such a major influence on the American colonists when they declared themselves independent of Great Britain?

4. **Summarize** What made the Declaration of Independence such a radical document?

5. **Draw Conclusions** If you were a colonial merchant in 1776, would you have supported the Declaration of Independence? Explain why or why not.

The American Revolution

6. **Summarize** In what ways did the French help the Americans against the British?

The United States Constitution

7. **Identify Cause and Effect** How did the ideas of the Enlightenment impact the U.S. Constitution's Bill of Rights?

8. **Summarize** Explain why the U.S. Constitution has been called a "progressive" document.

9. **Determine Meaning** Read the first paragraph of "Symbol of Freedom." What do you think the term *prototype* means in this context?

Lesson 6 The French Revolution Begins

CLOSE READING

The Old Regime in France

1. **Analyze Interactions** If you were a member of the Third Estate, how would your life be different from the life of a member of the Second Estate? Explain your answer.

2. **Cite Evidence** How did access to government differ among the First, Second, and Third Estates?

France's Economic Crisis

3. **Identify Cause and Effect** In what way was Louis XVI's attitude toward France's economic conditions a cause of the French Revolution?

Louis XVI Calls the Estates-General

4. **Draw Inferences** Why do you think the writings of Voltaire, Rousseau, and other *philosophes* influenced the members of the Third Estate more than those of the First and Second Estates?

Storming the Bastille

5. Summarize Describe the significance of the Bastille and the events of July 14, 1789.

Revolts in Paris and the Provinces

6. Summarize What were some of the major events of the "Great Fear"?

The National Assembly

7. Paraphrase When the National Assembly abolished feudalism, the president of the Assembly declared, **"We may view this moment as the dawn of a new revolution, when all the burdens weighing on the people were abolished, and France was truly reborn."** What do you think he meant?

8. Compare and Contrast In what ways did the American Revolution influence the French Revolution?

Reforms of the National Assembly

9. Draw Inferences What changes did the Constitution of 1791 bring to the French government? Which of these changes reflected the goals of the Enlightenment?

Lesson 7 A Radical Phase

CLOSE READING

Radicals Gain Strength

1. **Analyze Interactions** If you were a European monarch during the French Revolution, why would you fear the "French plague"?

2. **Compare and Contrast** Why did the political philosophy of the Jacobins throw the Revolution into another phase?

The Monarchy Is Abolished

3. **Paraphrase** Explain the meaning of the excerpt below from a statement given by King Louis XVI prior to his execution: "Frenchmen, I die innocent. I pardon the authors of my death. I pray God that the blood about to be spilt will never fall upon the head of France."

The Reign of Terror

4. **Draw Inferences** What was the result of Robespierre's desire to achieve a "republic of virtue"?

5. **Paraphrase** Explain in your own words what Robespierre meant when he said: "The first maxim of our politics ought to be to lead the people by means of reason and the enemies of the people by terror . . . If the basis of popular government in time of peace is virtue, the basis of popular government in time of revolution is both virtue and terror."

Reaction and the Directory

6. **Determine Central Ideas** What was the main impact of the Constitution of 1795?

The Revolution Transforms France

7. **Summarize** In what ways did the French Revolution change France?

8. **Compare and Contrast** How did the United States and France react differently to the role of religion in the state?

Lesson 8 The Age of Napoleon

CLOSE READING

Napoleon on the Rise

1. Draw Conclusions Napoleon once said: "Since one must take sides, one might as well choose the side that is victorious, the side which devastates, loots, and burns. Considering the alternative, it is better to eat than be eaten." What does this quote indicate about Napoleon's political ambitions and values?

2. Identify Cause and Effect How did Napoleon build his image as a military leader in France?

Napoleon Reforms France

3. Identify Cause and Effect Name at least three reforms Napoleon brought to France.

4. Compare and Contrast What did the Napoleonic Code have in common with the principles of the Enlightenment? How did Napoleon's rule violate Enlightenment principles?

The Napoleonic Wars

5. Draw Conclusions In the section titled, "Redrawing the Map of Europe," what does the text mean when it uses the term "forceful diplomacy"?

6. Summarize The Continental System did not work. Why?

Challenges to the French Empire

7. Summarize At first some Europeans welcomed Napoleon in their countries. Why did they eventually turn against him?

Napoleon Falls from Power

8. Analyze Interactions If you were a citizen of France in 1814, would you have welcomed Napoleon back from his exile? Explain your answer.

The Congress of Vienna

9. Analyze Interactions What were the major outcomes of the Congress of Vienna?

PRIMARY SOURCE EXPLORATION

Human Rights

Introduction

In 1948, the United Nations adopted the Universal Declaration of Human Rights. It was the first document to list rights to which everyone is entitled. Inspired partly by the American Declaration of Independence and the French Declaration of the Rights of Man and the Citizen, the Universal Declaration of Human Rights went further than either of the older documents. While it is not a legal document, it has provided the framework for international laws and constitutions supporting and protecting human rights. It remains the standard for those seeking principles to protect their rights. The pursuit of fully achieving those principles and the promised protection continues.

Document-Based Writing Activity

Analyze the following four sources and then use information from the documents and your knowledge of world history to write an essay in which you

- Describe some of the rights addressed in the United Nations Declaration of Human Rights. Were there earlier declarations of human rights?
- Discuss the changes in human rights since the United Nations Declaration in 1948. Why did these changes occur?

Keep in mind that your essay should include an introduction, several paragraphs, and a conclusion. In the body of the essay, use evidence from at least three documents. Support your response with relevant facts, examples, and details. In developing your essay, be sure to keep these general definitions in mind:

- *Describe* means "to illustrate something in words or tell about it."
- *Discuss* means "to make observations about something using facts, reasoning, and argument; to present in some detail."

Source 1

Is access to water a human right? This question was first posed at the conference at Mar del Plata in 1977. Since then, the issue has been both a national and an international matter. The conference was a success. An action plan was set in place. However, it was not until 2010 that the United Nations officially recognized clean drinking water and sanitation as a human right.

The United Nations Water Conference

I. Assessment of Water Resources

Recognizing that for the plans of action adopted by the Conference for the intensification and improvement of water use and development in agriculture and for all human settlements by 1990, a proper assessment is necessary of water resources in all countries of the world, and in particular in developing countries.

II. Community Water Supply

(a) All peoples, whatever their stage of development and their social and economic conditions, have the right to have access to drinking water in quantities and of a quality to their basic needs.

(b) It is universally recognized that the availability to man of that resource is essential both for life and his full development, both as an individual and as an integral part of society.

Recommends:

(a) That where human needs have not yet been satisfied, national development policies and plans should give priority to the supplying of drinking water for the entire population and to the final disposal of waste water; and should also actively involve, encourage and support efforts being undertaken by local voluntary organizations.

Plan of Action:

1. Action must focus on (a) increased awareness of the problem; (b) commitment of national Governments to provide all people with water of safe quality and adequate quantity and basic sanitary facilities by 1990 according priority to the poor and less privileged and to water scarce areas.......

---

1. According to this report, why is it necessary to make access to water a human right?

2. What was the suggested timetable for achieving the program's goals?

3. Which areas would be serviced first in the effort to meet the program goals? Why is this necessary?

Source 2

Malé Declaration on the Human Dimension of Global Climate Change, 2007

In 2007, a delegation from a group of small island nations met in Malé, the capital city of Maldives, to consider the effects of climate change. The result was the Malé Declaration which was the first time climate and global warming were addressed as factors in preventing "full enjoyment of human rights". The delegation appealed to the United Nations to consider the effect of global warming on human rights.

> We the representatives of the Small Island Developing States having met in Malé from 13 to 14 November 2007;
>
> Aware that the environment provides the infrastructure for human civilization and that life depends on the uninterrupted functioning of natural systems,
>
> Accepting the conclusions of the WMO/UNEP Intergovernmental Panel on Climate Change (IPCCC) including that climate change is … accelerating, and that … adaptation to climate change impacts is physically and economically feasible if urgent action is taken.
>
> Persuaded that the impacts of climate change pose the most immediate, fundamental and far-reaching threat to the environment, individuals and communities . . . and that these impacts have been observed to be intensifying in frequency. . . .
>
> Emphasizing that small island, low-lying coastal, and atoll states are particularly vulnerable to even small changes to the global climate and are already adversely affected by alterations in ecosystems, changes in precipitation, rising sea-levels and increase incidence of natural disasters.
>
> Concerned that climate change has clear and immediate implication for the full enjoyment of human rights, including. . .the right to life, the right to take part in cultural life, the right to use and enjoy property, the right to an adequate standard of living, the right to food, and the right to the highest attainable standard of physical and mental health.
>
> Do solemnly request the Office of the United Nations High Commissioner for Human Rights to conduct a detailed study into the effects of climate change on the full enjoyment of human rights . . . .

1. Explain the phrase "the environment provides for the infrastructure for human civilization". Why is this an important point in the presentation?

2. What evidence is presented to show that small island nations are more likely to suffer from climate change?

3. Why do you think the delegation saw this as a human rights issue?

Source 3

From the United Nations Human Rights report "The Right to Adequate Food"

The human right to food was a part of the UN Human Rights Declaration. It remains a challenge, both in developing and developed countries. The following is from a UN report on food rights.

The right to food is NOT the same as a right to be fed. Many assume that the right to food means that Governments have to hand out free food to anyone who needs it. They conclude that this would not be feasible (possible) or might cause dependency. This is a misunderstanding. The right to food is not a right to be fed, but primarily the right to feed oneself in dignity. Individuals are expected to meet their own needs, through their own efforts and using their own resources. To be able to do this, a person must live in conditions that allow him or her either to produce food or to buy it. To produce his or her own food, a person needs land, seeds, water and other resources, and to buy it, one needs money and access to the market. The right to food requires States to provide an enabling environment in which people can use their full potential to produce … adequate food for themselves and their families. However, when people are not able to feed themselves with their own means, for instance because of an armed conflict, natural disaster or because they are in detention, the State must provide food directly.

1. Based on the excerpt from the report, why is the right to be fed not recognized as a human right?

2. How might environmental conditions affect food availability?

3. Why is it necessary for the State to provide an "enabling environment"?

Source 4

2030 Agenda For Sustainable Development

In 2015, sixty-seven years after the UN Declaration of Human Rights, members of the UN set an agenda of goals which they hoped would result in an end to world poverty and improve quality of life. These goals, the sustainable development goals, are to be met by 2030.

As we enter the most pivotal decade for SDG {Sustainable Development Goals) implementation, the theme "Empowering People and Ensuring Inclusiveness and Equality" of the 2019 High-Level Political Forum for Sustainable Development couldn't be more timely.

Amongst the calls for more resources, more political will, more tools, technology and faster implementation, it is a reminder that equitable (a fair) and sustainable development must be achieved *with* and *not for* the people. Achieving the transformational promise of the SDGs depends on ensuring the empowerment, inclusion and equality of all people, which is so closely interconnected with human rights.

The promotion and protection of human rights is about empowering people to stand up for themselves and for each other, for equality, and for inclusive societies. This is how the power of human rights can foster and accelerate a transformative development agenda.

The SDGs already mirror much of the human rights framework. Each sustainable development goal, whether aimed at eradicating (ending) hunger, preventing disease, providing clean water . . . or focused on securing peace or decent work—all are simultaneously a claim about human rights.

Development is not just about changing the material conditions that prevent a person from reaching these goals. It is also about empowering people with voice and agency to be active participants in designing their own solutions and shaping development policy. It is about transforming laws, policy, practice, social norms, and power relations such that everyone can flourish in equal dignity and freedom.

This is recognized in the 2030 Agenda commitment to create "a world of universal respect for equality and non-discrimination". . . At its heart the Agenda 2030 promise of "leaving no one behind" is a reaffirmation that human rights and sustainable development are mutually reinforcing.

1. How do the Sustainable Goals build on the goals of the United Nations document?

2. Why is it important, in achieving goals, that it happens *with* the people rather than for the people?

3. What do you think the goal of not leaving anyone behind means?

Lesson 1 The Industrial Revolution Begins

CLOSE READING

New Ways of Working Change Life

1. **Compare and Contrast** As you read, fill out the graphic organizer below. In the graphic organizer, identify characteristics of how people lived before and after the Industrial Revolution.

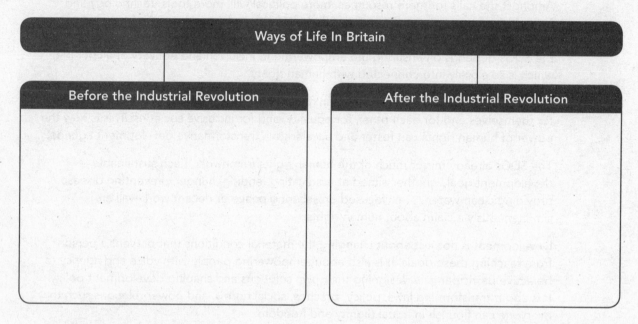

Ways of Life In Britain

Before the Industrial Revolution

After the Industrial Revolution

2. **Analyze Interactions** How did the Scientific Revolution of the seventeenth century lead to the Industrial Revolution?

A New Agricultural Revolution

3. **Identify Supporting Details** In what ways did a food surplus affect the population at the start of the Industrial Revolution?

Coal, Steam, and the Energy Revolution

4. Identify Cause and Effect How would steam engines improve industry?

Why Did the Industrial Revolution Start in Britain?

5. Summarize Explain how the four factors of production are each needed in order to produce goods.

Textile Industry Initiates Industrialization

6. Analyze Sequence Why did the flying shuttle require the invention of the spinning jenny?

A Revolution in Transportation

7. Analyze Sequence Review the text. Then describe the sequence of improvements in transportation, and explain how each improvement contributed to the Industrial Revolution.

Industrialization Spreads

8. Draw Inferences After the new inventions of the textile industry reached the United States, what advantages did the United States have over Britain?

Lesson 2 Social Impact of Industrialism

CLOSE READING

Industry Causes Urban Growth

1. **Draw Conclusions** What local characteristics were most likely to make towns and villages grow in population during the Industrial Revolution?

The Rise of New Social Classes

2. **Compare and Contrast** What was life like for the middle class compared to the working class?

Harsh Conditions in Factories and Mines

3. **Explain an Argument** Why do you think child labor was considered acceptable during the Industrial Revolution?

Benefits of the Industrial Revolution

4. **Analyze Interactions** Reread the text under the heading "Better Standards of Living." Explain the relationship between price and supply, and how this affected people's standard of living during the Industrial Revolution.

Laissez-Faire Economics

5. Vocabulary: Use Context Clues Why does "laissez-faire" describe free-enterprise capitalism?

Utilitarians Support Limited Government

6. Vocabulary: Determine Meaning Identify words that have a root word similar to that of *utilitarianism*. How are the definitions of these words related?

Socialist Thought Emerges

7. Determine Central Ideas What was Robert Owen's main goal in setting up a Utopian community at New Lanark?

Marx and the Origins of Communism

8. Draw Inferences Why did workers fail to unite and form successful communist societies?

Lesson 3 The Second Industrial Revolution

CLOSE READING

Science and Technology Change Industry

1. **Identify Cause and Effect** As you read "Science and Technology Change Industry," use this graphic organizer to list the inventions and new methods under causes, and then record the effects of each one.

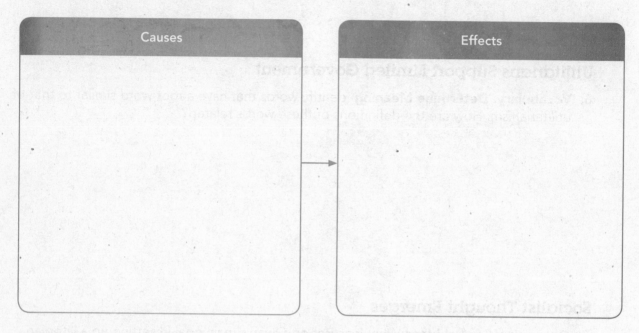

Causes	Effects

Advances in Transportation and Communication

2. **Draw Inferences** Why did industrialized nations build transcontinental railroads? How did expanding railroads affect the economy and people's way of life?

3. **Identify Cause and Effect** How did advances in communication impact the world and the economy during the Industrial Revolution? Which inventions continue to impact business and society?

The Rise of Big Business

4. **Determine Central Ideas** How did big businesses emerge?

5. **Explain an Argument** Why was there a debate over the growth of big business? Explain both sides of the argument. Cite textual evidence to support your response.

Better Medicine, Nutrition, and Health

6. **Identify Cause and Effect** Identify some of the medical advances of the late 1800s. What impact did these medical advances have on human life?

City Life Changes

7. **Draw Conclusions** Why was the spread of disease a problem in industrial cities in the mid-1800s? What changes did people make to try to stop epidemics?

The Working Class Wins New Rights

8. **Draw Conclusions** Why was it important that workers won the right to organize unions? How did this right affect working conditions?

Lesson 4 Changing Ways of Life and Thought

CLOSE READING

The New Social Order

1. **Determine Central Ideas** How did the Industrial Revolution change the social order in the Western world?

The Struggle for Women's Rights

2. **Summarize** Why was it difficult for women to gain political rights during the 1800s? Why were women able to acquire the vote in some regions?

The Rise of Public Education

3. **Draw Inferences** What skills did schools begin to teach beyond academics? Why did they begin teaching these skills?

New Directions in Science

4. **Determine Central Ideas** What new sciences and discoveries challenged long-held beliefs about the age of the Earth? Why were these ideas controversial?

The Role of Religion

5. **Draw Inferences** Why did living conditions in industrialized nations encourage compassionate and charitable feelings among some people?

The Romantics Turn from Reason

6. **Make Inferences** What themes inspired many romantic writers and architects? Why might they have found these ideas inspirational?

Artists Represent Real Life

7. **Draw Conclusions** What subjects did realist writers typically focus on in their novels? Why did they focus on these people and things?

New Directions in Visual Arts

8. **Compare and Contrast** How does impressionist painting differ from realist painting?

PRIMARY SOURCE EXPLORATION

Impact of the Industrial Revolution

Introduction

The industrial revolution which began in eighteenth century Britain changed not only the economy but nearly every other aspect of British society and life. As industrialization slowly spread, after 1850, to Europe, the United States, and the rest of the world, the impact of new political, economic, and social developments changed the way people lived and the way nations co-existed.

Document-Based Writing Activity

Analyze the following four sources and then use information from the documents and your knowledge of world history to write an essay in which you

- Describe how the industrial revolution impacted Britain.
- Discuss the global impact of the industrial revolution outside Britain.

Keep in mind that your essay should include an introduction, several paragraphs, and a conclusion. In the body of the essay, use evidence from at least three documents. Support your response with relevant facts, examples, and details. In developing your essay, be sure to keep these general definitions in mind:

- *Describe* means "to illustrate something in words or tell about it."
- *Discuss* means "to make observations about something using facts, reasoning, and argument; to present in some detail."

Source 1

"The Cockerills of Liège" from the Journal Iron, *1839*

Before the industrial revolution, Belgium had economic advantages. Textile production flourished along with the beginnings of coal and iron industries. In 1799, William Cockerill, an Englishman, installed the first spinning machine in Verviers, a city in Belgium. Cockerill recounts the road to building his business.

Along with some other skillful mechanics, he proceeded, by the permission of our government, to St. Petersburgh, with the view of following out certain plans of Empress Catherine for establishing manufacturers in her domain. The death of the Empress, and the accession of [Paul I] ruined his prospects in Russia and after a time [he] made his escape to Sweden. (Cockerill) under the protection of the British envoy. . . was employed as an engineer of public works, which no native Swedes could undertake. Engineering however did not suit his genius, and hearing of manufacturers of Liège and Verviers in Belgium which were flourishing in spite of defective mechanism, he imagined that if he were in either of these places he would be certain to succeed as a constructor of machines. He proceeded first, as we were told, to Hamburg, where he disclosed the plans of his proposed operation to Mr. Crawford, the English consul, at the same time saying "that if he could obtain a small pension from the British Government, he would return to England, not wishing to do injury to his country by introducing machinery to a foreign one." Mr. Crawford, it appears, approved of the proposal, and communicated it to the ministry, but no answer being returned at the end of six months, Cockerill proceeded to the Netherlands, there to seek fortune with his own head and hands.

He made offers to some extensive woolen manufacturers of Verviers, a town within the province of Liège, to construct for them new machines of his own invention for the carding and spinning of wool, and for other purposes connected with the production of cloth fabrics. The offers were accepted, and William Cockerill forthwith brought his family from England, and settled them in Belgium. Cockerill's sons were now growing up, and with the assistance of their hands and his own, he speedily executed all orders, and founded a thriving establishment. The workshop of the Cockerills at Liège became a famous one, and the quantity of machines made for various manufacturers was soon considerable.

---

1. Why did Cockerill have to change his plans for starting a business in Russia?

2. Why do you think the British were willing to consider Cockerill's proposal?

3. How did Cockerill's business affect the economy of Belgium?

Source 2

A Petition by Eli Whitney to the U.S. Congress, Requesting Renewal of His Cotton Gin Patent, 1812

The first patent for Eli Whitney's cotton gin was granted in 1794. The invention was successful. It was also easy to duplicate and many farmers stole the idea and made their own version. The first patent ended in 1807. Whitney appeals to Congress for a renewal.

Permit your memorialist [a person who petitions or makes a request] further to remark that by far the greatest part of the cotton raised in the United States has been and must of necessity continue to be the Green Seed. That, before the invention of your memorialist, the value of this species of cotton after it was cleaned was not equal to the expense of cleaning it. That since the cultivation of this species has been a great source of wealth to the community and of riches to thousands of her citizens. That as a labor-saving machine it is an invention which enables one man to perform in a given time that which would require a thousand men without its aid to perform in the same time. In short that it furnished to the whole family of mankind the means of procuring [getting] the article of cotton, that important raw material, which constitutes a great part of their clothing at a much cheaper rate.

Your memorialist begs leave further to state that a confident expectation that his case would be embraced in the general law which Congress has for several years had under its ideation [consideration] has prevented his making an earlier application. That the expenses incurred by him in making and introducing this useful improvement and establishing his claim to its invention, have absorbed great proportion of what he has received, from those states with which he has made a compromise. That he humbly conceives himself fairly entitled to a further remuneration [payment] from his Country—and that he ought to be admitted to a more liberal participation with his fellow citizens, in the benefits of his invention. . .

He therefore prays your Honourable Body to take his case into consideration and authorize the renewal of his Patent or grant such other relief, as Congress in their wisdom and their justice may deem meet and proper [find appropriate].

1. How does Whitney justify the renewal of the patent for his cotton gin?

2. Aside from a renewal, what else is Whitney requesting?

3. What do you think were the social and economic effects of this invention?

Source 3

"Cotton in India" Illustrated London News, January 21, 1854

The growth of industrialization led to an increase in demand for raw materials and markets to sell goods. This, along with other factors, resulted in imperialism. Britain, like most industrialized nations at the time, established colonies in Africa and Asia to gain access to raw materials and new markets. This new imperialism led to the British presence in India in the eighteenth century.

Hitherto, we have maintained ourselves in India by the strong arm; but it is beginning to be recognized by the inhabitants of India that our Government has, upon the whole, been beneficial to their country, and that a movement has at last been made for the development of its material resources, which it would be vain for them to expect, if the English were driven out of India, and a native or alien government established in their stead [place]. In a country so vast and so fertile, it is impossible to predict what great summit of prosperity may not be attained [how much wealth can be gained] during the next twelve or twenty years, if railroads are constructed, as in all probability they will be, to connect all the principal towns and cities, and if its great agricultural wealth shall thereby be transmitted with cheapness and regularity from province to province, and from every part of the interior to the sea-coast. Long before the present difficulty arose between Russia and the Ports, the busy but thoughtful men of Manchester were of opinion that much and lasting benefit would accrue [come] both to England and to India, if we could draw a portion, if not the whole, of our supplies of cotton from that magnificent dependency. If India supplies us annually with only half as much cotton as we now import from the United States, we should have a security for the permanency of our power quite as valid, and far more profitable, than the armies that we have hitherto been obliged to maintain.

---

1. Explain the phrase "maintained ourselves in India by the strong arm."

2. How does Great Britain justify their presence in India?

3. What disruptions might the inhabitants of India have felt from British military presence?

Source 4

A railway between Tokyo and Yokohama, 1875

One result of the Meiji Restoration of 1868 was the westernization of Japan. Early accomplishments of Japan's industrialization included changes in transportation. The first railway link between Tokyo and Yokohama opened in the early 1870s. Below is an image of the railway.

1. Based on this picture, what was the main method of transport before railroads?

2. How did industrialization begin to affect Japan?

3. The government was eager to expand railroads. Do you think there may have been opposition to this move? Explain.

Lesson 1 Revolutions Sweep Europe

CLOSE READING

A Clash of Ideologies

1. **Determine Central Ideas** Explain what Prince Metternich meant by "the revolutionary seed." Cite evidence from the text to support your answer.

Liberalism and Nationalism Spur Revolts

2. **Determine Central Ideas** As you read "A Clash of Ideologies" and "Liberals and Nationalists Spur Revolts," use this graphic organizer to list the characteristics of conservatism, liberalism, and nationalism.

Liberalism	Nationalism	Conservatism
•	•	•
•	•	•
•	•	•
•	•	•
•	•	•

Rebellions Erupt in Eastern Europe

3. **Compare** How were the revolts in Serbia, Greece, Spain, Portugal, and the Italian states similar? What ideals did the revolutionaries have in common?

Revolutions of 1830 and 1848

4. **Identify Cause and Effect** Explain the causes that led to the French Revolution of 1830.

Demands for Reform Spread

5. Compare and Contrast Fill in the Venn diagram below with information about the Belgian and Polish uprisings. What factor most affected the outcome of the two revolutions?

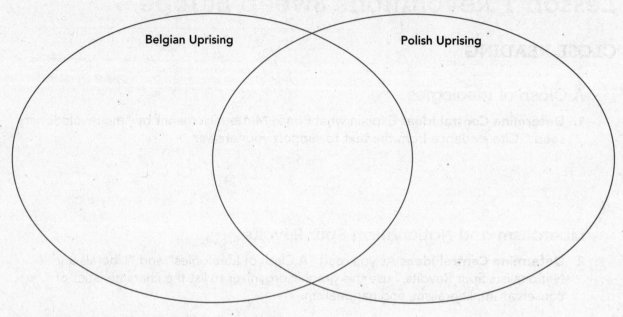

Belgian Uprising

Polish Uprising

The Revolution of 1848 in France

6. Compare and Contrast How were the "February Days" and the "June Days" similar and different?

7. Draw Inferences The revolutions of 1830 and 1848 were the result of new ways of thinking and hard times for workers. Could one of these factors by itself have caused such widespread rebellion? Why or why not?

Revolution Spreads Across Europe

8. Draw Conclusions Why were most of the rebellions in 1848 unsuccessful?

Lesson 2 Latin American Nations Win Independence

CLOSE READING

Spanish America Rises Up

1. **Draw Conclusions** How did the American Revolution impact the revolutions in Latin America?

Haiti Fights for Freedom

2. **Identify Supporting Details** What led enslaved Haitians to revolt and fight with Toussaint L'Ouverture for independence?

3. **Draw Conclusions** How might the Haitian Revolution have ended if French soldiers had not had to battle yellow fever?

Revolts in Mexico and Central America

4. **Identify Supporting Details** Fill in the chart below with details about how these revolutionary leaders helped to free Mexico and Central America.

Father Miguel Hidalgo	Father José Morelos	Agustín de Iturbide

5. Compare How did Iturbide's motive for rebellion differ from the motives of Father Hidalgo and Father Morelos?

6. Cause and Effect How did events in Spain affect the fight for Mexican independence?

Discontent Sparks Revolts in South America

7. Draw Conclusions Why was Bolívar's plan to march his army across the Andes considered daring? Why did this daring plan succeed?

8. Evaluate Explanations What did Bolívar mean when he wrote, "We achieved our independence at the expense of everything else"?

Lesson 3 The Unification of Germany

CLOSE READING

Moving Toward a Unified Germany

1. **Draw Conclusions** How did Napoleon's invasions affect Germany?

Bismarck Becomes the Architect of German Unity

2. **Identify Supporting Details** Explain how Bismarck's persistence in strengthening the Prussian army helped to unify Germany.

3. **Draw Conclusions** How did the emperor and his chancellor retain power in the new German government?

Germany Becomes an Industrial Giant

4. **Identify Supporting Details** What factors allowed Germany to grow into an industrial giant?

5. **Identify Cause and Effect** How did the German government support economic development?

The Iron Chancellor

6. **Determine Central Ideas** Identify the origins of socialism in Germany.

7. **Analyze Word Choices** Why was Bismarck known as the "Iron Chancellor"?

Kaiser William II

8. **Compare and Contrast** List two ways that Bismarck and Kaiser William II were similar and one way they were different.

Lesson 4 The Unification of Italy

CLOSE READING

First Steps to Italian Unity

1. **Determine Author's Point of View** What did Mazzini mean by this quote: "Ideas grow quickly when watered by the blood of martyrs"?

2. **Categorize** List the geographic, cultural, and economic reasons for Italian unification.

The Struggle for Italy

3. **Compare and Contrast** How were the views of Cavour, Mazzini, and Garibaldi alike? How were they different?

4. **Analyze Interactions** Why did Sardinia ally itself first with France and then, later, with Prussia against France?

5. Draw Inferences Why did Garibaldi give Naples and Sicily to Victor Emmanuel?

Italy Faces New Challenges

6. Compare and Contrast Use the graphic organizer below to compare and contrast the regional differences of northern and southern Italy.

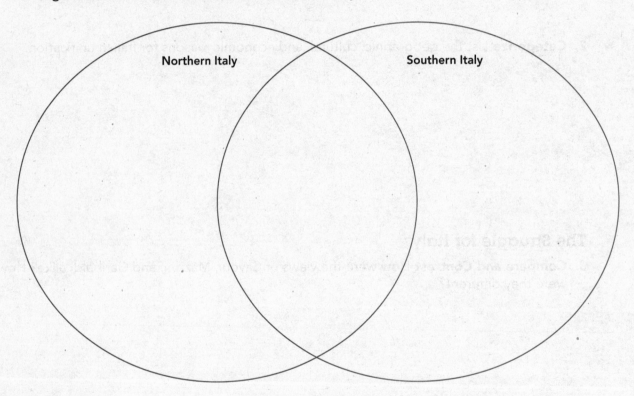

Northern Italy   Southern Italy

7. Cite Evidence How did the Italian government try to contain political unrest in the late 1800s?

Lesson 5 Democratic Reforms in Britain

CLOSE READING

Two Nations

1. **Draw Conclusions** Why would expanding democratic rights help to bridge Britain's "two nations"?

2. **Summarize** How did the Great Reform Act of 1832 change Parliament?

The Victorian Age

3. **Categorize** What values did Queen Victoria represent, and how did these values relate to economic reform?

Reforms Increase Parliamentary Democracy

4. **Summarize** Why did the House of Lords eventually become a largely ceremonial body with little power?

Economic and Social Reforms

5. Determine Central Issues How did abolition and criminal justice reform reflect Victorian values?

Victories for the Working Class

6. Cite Evidence Look through the text of the lesson to find examples of three reforms that helped the British working class. Use details to describe each one and the groups affected.

Women Struggle for the Vote

7. Analyze Interactions Why do you think women disagreed about how best to gain suffrage?

The Irish Question

8. Determine Central Ideas How did British policies toward Ireland affect the cause of Irish nationalism?

Lesson 6 Divisions and Democracy in France

CLOSE READING

Napoleon III and the Second Empire

1. Identify Supporting Details For what reasons did a wide variety of French people support Napoleon III?

2. Summarize What were some of Napoleon III's political reforms?

3. Cite Evidence What actions did Mexican patriots take during Napoleon III's rule?

The Third Republic Faces New Struggles

4. Cite Evidence In what ways did the Communards hope to change their government?

5. Synthesize Why were there 50 different governments in the first 10 years of the Third Republic?

The Dreyfus Affair

6. Draw Inferences What did the Dreyfus Affair reveal about French society?

Reforms in France

7. Identify Supporting Details How did Republicans view the influence of the Church?

8. Cite Evidence What is one possible reason that French women did not get the vote until after World War II? Use information from the text to support your answer.

Lesson 7 Growth of the United States

CLOSE READING

The United States Expands

1. **Identify Cause and Effect** What is expansionism, and how did a policy of expansionism affect the United States?

Expanding Democracy

2. **Cite Evidence** Describe how the electorate changed during the 1800s. Be sure to cite dates from the text.

3. **Determine Central Ideas** How was the issue of slavery connected to the expansion of the United States?

4. **Analyze Interactions** How did involvement in the abolition movement help launch the fight for women's rights?

The Civil War

5. **Identify Cause and Effect** What were the main differences between the Northern and Southern states, and what ultimately caused the Southern states to secede from the Union?

6. **Summarize** Look at the infographic and summarize the post-Civil War amendments.

Economic Growth and Reform

7. **Explain** What factors helped the United States become an agricultural and industrial leader? Choose one factor and explain its influence.

8. **Identify Supporting Details** How did the Populist Party influence reform in the United States?

Lesson 8 Nationalism in Eastern Europe and Russia

CLOSE READING

Nationalism Endangers Old Empires

1. **Identify Cause and Effect** Why did industrialization challenge the rule of the Hapsburgs, and what was the result?

The Dual Monarchy

2. **Draw Inferences** Why was the Dual Monarchy an insufficient compromise?

The Ottoman Empire Declines

3. **Draw Inferences** Why was the Ottoman Empire called the "sick man of Europe"?

Russia Tries Reform

4. **Analyze Interactions** Describe the different levels in Russian society and their interactions with one another.

Emancipation and Stirrings of Revolution

5. Determine Central Ideas What event was the catalyst for reform during Alexander II's reign, and what did it show?

6. Summarize What was "Russification," and what was its effect?

The Beginnings of Industrialization

7. Draw Inferences Why did radicals find "fertile ground" in Russia in the late nineteenth and early twentieth centuries?

The Road to Revolution

8. Determine Central Ideas Why did Stolypin's reforms fail to ease the tension in Russia?

PRIMARY SOURCE EXPLORATION

Nationalism Versus Democracy in Germany

Introduction

By the mid-1800s, the spread of democracy across Europe had reached southern Germany, where constitutional monarchies with powerful elected parliaments developed. Prussia, to the north, had an elected parliament, but votes were weighted by wealth, so that wealthier Prussians controlled the parliament. Laws passed by the parliament could be vetoed by an unelected House of Lords—made up mainly of nobles and prominent people appointed by the king—or by the king himself. The king appointed all government ministers. The Prussian nobility also dominated the kingdom's powerful army. Prussia's king and nobility grew determined to unify Germany by force and to limit the role of democracy in the newly united country.

Document-Based Writing Activity

Analyze the following four sources and then use information from the documents and your knowledge of world history to write an essay in which you

- Compare and contrast the arguments used by proponents of democracy and proponents of unification by force.
- Describe how Germany's unification came at the expense of democracy.

Keep in mind that your essay should include an introduction, several paragraphs, and a conclusion. In the body of the essay, use evidence from at least three documents. Support your response with relevant facts, examples, and details. In developing your essay, be sure to keep these general definitions in mind:

- *Compare* means "to find similarities between two ideas or documents."
- *Contrast* means "to find differences between two ideas or documents."
- *Describe* means "to illustrate something in words or tell about it."

Source 1

Proposal of Gustav von Struve to the Frankfurt Pre-Parliament, March 31, 1848

In Germany as in much of Europe, the Revolution of 1848 was a movement for democracy. In this speech to a meeting organizing Germany's first real parliament, Gustav von Struve outlines a set of democratic goals. Though Prussian troops suppressed the revolution in 1849, these goals continued to inspire German democrats.

A long time under the deepest humiliation weighs on Germany. It can be described in these words: enslavement, dumbing down, and exploitation for the people; arbitrary rule, riches, and honors for the rulers and their henchmen. Under the influence of this system of tyranny . . . Germany has more than once been brought to the brink of ruin. . . .

Security of property and personal safety, prosperity, education, and freedom for all, regardless of birth, social class, or religion are the goals toward which the German people strive. The means to achieve them are:

1) Dissolution of the standing armies and their merger with the citizens' militia in order to form a true people's army comprising all men capable of bearing weapons. . . .

4) Elimination of all privileges . . . especially of the nobility, the privileges of wealth, the right to privileged courts of law, and their replacement with a civil law applicable to all. . . .

8) Elimination of censorship . . . and [its] replacement . . . with the principle of full freedom of the press.

12) Leveling of the unfair relationship between labor [workers] and capital [business owners] by means of a special department of labor, which regulates profiteering and protects labor and specifically insures for [workers] a share of profits.

14) Elimination of the division of Germany . . .

15) Dissolution of hereditary monarchy (autocracy) and its replacement with freely elected parliaments, led by freely elected presidents, united only by a federal constitution modeled after that of the [United States].

German people, these are the only principles under which in our opinion Germany can become happy, respected, and free. German brothers in east and west, we call on you to support us in the effort to obtain for you these eternal and unchanging human rights! . . . Meanwhile, we will prepare . . . the great work of rebuilding Germany.

---

1. What disadvantages has Germany faced, according to what Struve states or implies?

2. How does he want to correct the problems he identifies?

3. How does he think Germany should be unified, and what are his reasons for wanting that form of unification?

Source 2

"Blood and Iron," speech by Chancellor Otto von Bismarck, September 30, 1862

In 1862, the king of Prussia wanted a larger military budget. Prussia's constitution gave the Prussian House of Representatives the right to approve spending. They refused the king's wishes. In this speech, the Prussian chancellor appointed by the king, Otto von Bismarck, explains why he will ignore this part of Prussia's constitution.

The conflict will probably still be resolved in a constitutional way, or rather, we will hopefully end up fitting the constitution better to the Prussian body. Violations of the constitution are not simple math problems; they can be solved only with mutual consideration. The great independence of the individual makes it difficult in Prussia to govern with the constitution. It's different in France; this individual independence is missing there. A constitutional crisis is no cause for shame, but an honor. Indeed, we are perhaps "too educated" to handle a constitution; we are too critical; the ability to judge government measures or acts of parliament is too common; there are too many [rebellious people] who have an interest in upheaval. It may sound strange, but everything shows how difficult constitutional living is in Prussia. Public opinion changes . . . representatives [in the Prussian House of Representatives] should have the greater task of setting the mood, of standing above it. Once more regarding our people: we have blood that is too hot, we have a penchant for carrying too much armor for our thin body . . . It isn't Prussia's liberalism that Germany is watching, but its power; Bavaria, Württemberg, or Baden [independent states in southern Germany] may indulge liberalism; but no one would assign them Prussia's role. Prussia must gather together its power in its grip for the opportune moment, which has already been missed several times. Prussia's borders after [the Congress of] Vienna [which ended the Napoleonic Wars in 1815 and left Prussia divided into separate territories] are not suited to a healthy state order. It is not with speeches and majority resolutions that the great questions of the time [such as German unification] will be decided—that was the mistake of 1848 and 1849—but rather with iron and blood.

1. According to Bismarck, why is it impossible to govern with a constitution in Prussia?

2. Why does he argue that liberalism is inappropriate for Prussia?

3. How does he justify the king's demand for greater military spending? What does he mean by "iron and blood"?

Source 3

"On the Constitution of the North German Confederation," speech by Johann Jacoby, May 6, 1867

In 1866, Prussia challenged Austria and its allies in the Austro-Prussian War. Prussia conquered much of northern Germany and created a new federal state, the North German Confederation, combining Prussia with several smaller states. In this speech, Prussian democrat Johann Jacoby opposes the constitution of the Confederation, which would give Prussia's king even greater power to overrule elected parliaments.

My dear sirs! . . . The draft constitution under consideration for the North German Confederation abolishes the essential constitutional rights of the Prussian people; therefore, I reject it. What I pronounced in this assembly a few weeks ago—that the military deeds of the Prussian army will help neither freedom nor the German fatherland— has already been too soon fulfilled.

. . .[Y]ou are now asked to do without your constitutional rights [as Prussians] . . . for the sake of absolute rule. . . .

I consider it my duty to bear witness to my contemporaries and those who come after that there are still men among the Prussian people . . . who are not willing to sacrifice constitutional rights such as freedom to the illusions of national power and honor.

. . . My dear sirs! Allow me as one of the oldest fighters for a constitutional state in Prussia, allow me in closing one short word of warning. Do not deceive yourselves about the results of your resolution [to approve the North German Constitution]! Limiting rights and freedoms has never led a people to national power and greatness.

Give the "supreme military commander" [the emperor] absolute power, and you declare at the same time war between peoples! Germany—united freely—is the surest guaranty for the peace of Europe; under Prussian military domination, however, Germany is a lasting danger for the neighboring peoples, the beginning of an era of war, that threatens to throw us back to the dismal times of the law of the jungle. May Prussia, may the German fatherland remain protected against such a sad fate!

1. How does Jacoby's view differ from Bismarck's?

2. Why does Jacoby see the constitution as a loss for Prussians and Germans?

3. What consequences does Jacoby foresee from Prussia's forcible unification of German lands?

Source 4

Painting of William I being crowned German Kaiser in the Palace of Versailles, 1871

In 1870, Prussia did as Jacoby had feared and launched a war with France. The southern German states joined Prussia to defeat France. In this painting, Prussia's king, William I, is crowned emperor of all of Germany in France's Palace of Versailles. Just as Jacoby feared, a Prussian-dominated Germany would go on to fight its neighbors in World War I.

1. How does the scene in this image back up the claims Bismarck made in his "Iron and Blood" speech?

2. How does this scene justify Jacoby's fears?

3. What does the scene suggest about the nature of power in newly unified Germany?

Lesson 1 The New Imperialism

CLOSE READING

Motivations for the New Imperialism

1. **Identify Cause and Effect** As you read "Motivations for the New Imperialism," use this graphic organizer to record multiple causes of the New Imperialism.

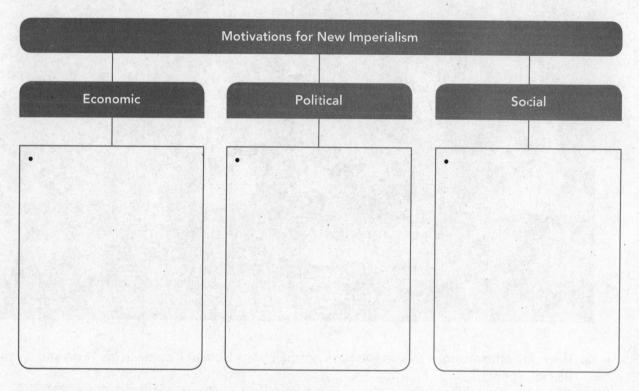

Western Imperialism Spreads Rapidly

2. **Identify Supporting Details** What details under "Western Advantages" support the idea that superior weaponry helped Western imperialism spread?

3. **Draw Inferences** Why did some Africans and Asians fight Western imperialism, even though they lacked powerful weapons like the Maxim gun?

Types of Imperial Rule

4. **Compare and Contrast** How was setting up a protectorate different from practicing direct rule?

5. **Draw Conclusions** Why did European countries sometimes choose to maintain spheres of influence instead of creating colonies?

The Effects of Imperialism

6. **Identify Cause and Effect** As European power spread, so did European ideas. What European ideas led to colonial resistance?

7. **Draw Inferences** What problems might an outside country create if it draws borders without understanding local political or ethnic situations?

Lesson 2 European Colonies in Africa

CLOSE READING

Africa Before Imperialism

1. **Predict Consequences** What was the state of the Ottoman empire in the early 1800s? How might that influence events in North Africa?

2. **Compare and Contrast** conditions in West Africa to those in East Africa in the early 1800s.

3. **Analyze Interactions** How did the fact that the British took control of Cape Colony in Southern Africa affect developments in the region?

European Contact Increases

4. **Cite Evidence** Why did the first Europeans to travel into the interior of Africa make the journey?

European Nations Scramble for Colonies

5. **Identify Cause and Effect** As you read "European Nations Scramble for Colonies," examine the text for major instances of imperialism and their effects. Then use a chart like this one to record some of the effects of European imperialism in Africa.

Cause	Effect
King Leopold II/Belgium in the Congo	
France in North, West, and Central Africa	
Britain in southern and eastern Africa	
Portugal, Italy, and Germany	

6. **Predict Consequences** According to the text, missionaries wanted to help Africans and thought that expanding Western influence into the interior of the continent would improve life for Africans. How do you think these missionaries would have reacted to King Leopold II's rule of the Congo?

African Resistance

7. **Identify Steps in a Process** What steps did Menelik II take to successfully resist Italian conquest?

Lesson 3 Europe and the Muslim World

CLOSE READING

Unrest in Muslim Regions

1. **Identify Cause and Effect** as you read "Unrest in Muslim Regions." Fill in a chart like this one below showing the causes of unrest in Muslim regions during the 1700s and 1800s.

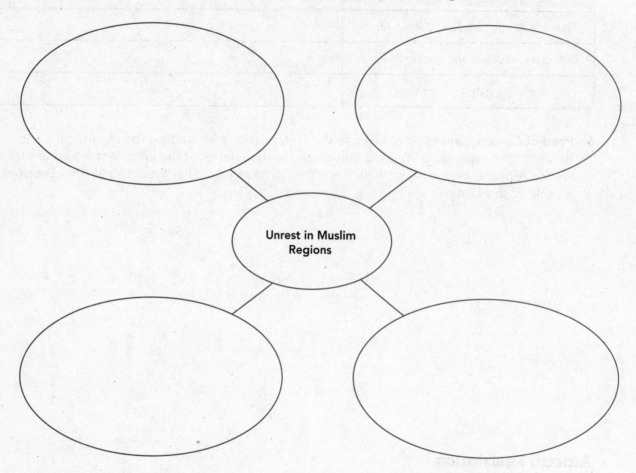

Unrest in Muslim Regions

2. **Draw Inferences** Why would Muhammad Ahmad be especially effective at leading resistance against the British?

The Ottoman Empire Declines

3. **Analyze Information** How did geography play a part in European interest in Muslim regions?

4. **Identify Central Issues** What role did nationalism play in the Armenian genocide?

Modernization in Egypt

5. **Infer** Why do you think Muhammad Ali was able to conquer Arabia, Syria, and Sudan?

6. **Analyze Interactions** Why did the Ottoman empire allow Britain to dictate policies in Egypt?

European Imperialism in Persia

7. **Analyze Interactions** How did the reasons for Russian and British interests in Persia change?

8. **Draw Conclusions** Why might two groups of Persian nationalists have such different views on how Persia should respond to Western imperialism?

Lesson 4 India Becomes a British Colony

CLOSE READING

The British East India Company

1. **Identify Cause and Effect** As you read "The British East India Company," examine the text for clues that signal cause and effect. Then use a chart like this one to record major causes and effects of British colonial rule in India.

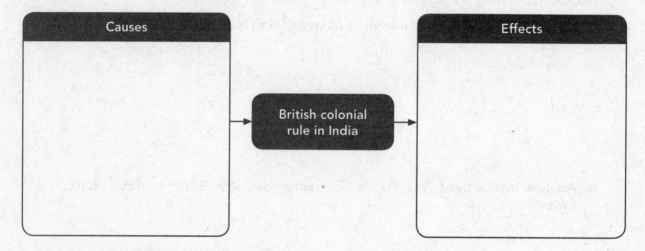

Causes

British colonial rule in India

Effects

2. **Analyze Interactions** How did the British react to the diversity of the people in India?

3. **Analyze Interactions** How did a lack of cultural understanding contribute to the Uprising of 1857?

India Under British Rule

4. **Draw Conclusions** Why would machine-made textiles from Britain ruin India's hand-weaving industry?

5. **Cite Evidence** from the text for the argument that India grew more unified under British rule.

Diverse Views on Culture

6. **Cite Evidence** Why is Ram Mohun Roy called the founder of Indian nationalism?

The Growth of Indian Nationalism

7. **Compare and Contrast** the Muslim League to the Indian National Congress.

8. **Evaluate** Why did British imperialists think Western education would benefit both Indians and the British? In what way were they mistaken?

Lesson 5 China and the West

CLOSE READING

Economic Interest in China

1. Cite Evidence Why was Britain eager to have China buy products from western countries as well as sell products to them?

2. Identify Cause and Effect As you read "Economic Interest in China," examine the text for clues that signal how British intervention affected China. Then use a chart like this one to record major effects.

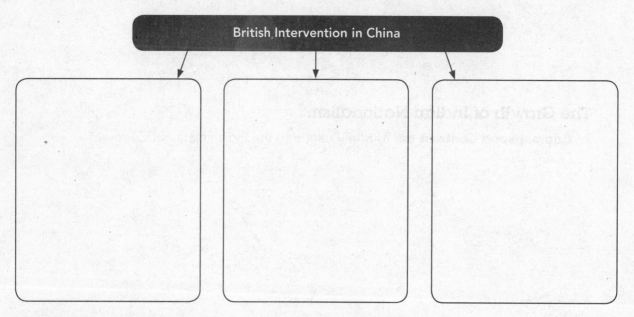

British Intervention in China

The Taiping Rebellion and a Weakened China

3. Identify Supporting Details What details under "The Taiping Rebellion and a Weakened China" support the idea that China was weaker when the rebellion took place than it had been in earlier times?

4. **Draw Inferences** Why do you think the Qing dynasty had to share power with regional commanders after the Taiping Rebellion?

Reform Efforts in China

5. **Draw Conclusions** Why did the Chinese government refuse to support the self-strengthening movement?

6. **Draw Conclusions** Why was the Open Door Policy advantageous to the United States?

The Fall of the Qing Dynasty

7. **Summarize** What led to resentment of foreigners living in China in the late 1800s and early 1900s?

8. **Identify Causes and Effects** What were the effects of the Boxer Uprising?

Lesson 6 The Modernization of Japan

CLOSE READING

Unrest in Tokugawa Japan

1. **Identify Cause and Effect** What were major causes and effects of the decline of Tokugawa Japan?

The Opening of Japan

2. **Hypothesize** Why do you think the United States approached Japan in the way it did, *demanding* that Japan open the door to trade and diplomacy?

3. **Draw Conclusions** How did Japan's adaptation to Western ways help balance its relationship with Western countries?

Transformation During the Meiji Period

4. **Compare and Contrast** Compare and contrast Japan before and during the Meiji Restoration.

5. **Cite Evidence** What evidence in the text supports the claim that Japan successfully updated its industries during the Meiji Restoration?

6. **Summarize** During the Meiji Restoration, many changes were made to the hierarchical class system in Japan. What inequalities remained?

Japan Builds an Empire

7. **Compare and Contrast** how Japan and Korea dealt with imperialistic ambitions of other countries.

8. **Summarize** How did Japan gain rule over Korea?

Lesson 7 Southeast Asia and the Pacific

CLOSE READING

European Imperialism in Southeast Asia

1. **Determine Central Ideas** What is the main reason the Dutch and British colonized areas of Southeast Asia? Cite evidence from the text to support your answer.

2. **Summarize** Read "The French in Indochina." What seems to be the main reason the French colonized Vietnam?

3. **Draw Inferences** How did the unequal treaties that Siam made with Western powers keep it independent and free from colonization?

Military Might and the Philippines

4. **Identify Cause and Effect** Why were Filipinos like Emilio Aguinaldo disappointed by the treaty that ended the Spanish-American War?

Strategic Holdings in the Pacific Islands

5. Summarize Why were Western countries interested in the islands of the Pacific?

6. Draw Inferences Why did the Hawaiian queen Liliuokalani want to reduce the influence of foreigners, particularly American sugar growers?

Europeans in Australia

7. Identify Cause and Effect Why did Australian colonies unite into a commonwealth? Why was this in Britain's best interest?

New Zealand's Story

8. Compare and Contrast How was the experience of the Maori similar to and different from that of the Australian Aborigines when white settlers arrived?

9. Draw Conclusions Why did New Zealanders preserve close ties with the British empire?

Lesson 8 The Americas in the Age of Imperialism

CLOSE READING

Political Problems Linger

1. **Hypothesize** How might Latin America have developed after colonialism if Simón Bolívar's dream had come true?

2. **Summarize** Why did Latin American countries have a difficult time adopting democracy?

Mexico's Search for Stability

3. **Compare** Benito Juárez and General Porfirio Díaz were very different rulers. Regardless, both helped to stabilize Mexico. What did each do to help stabilize the country? What were the advances each made?

The Economics of Latin America's Dependence

4. **Summarize** How did the policies of ruling governments prevent former colonies from developing their own economies?

5. Identify Cause and Effect What were some positive effects of foreign investment in Latin America?

The United States Wields Power and Influence

6. Cite Evidence What statement did the Monroe Doctrine make to the rest of the world? Cite evidence from the text to support your answer.

7. Identify Cause and Effect How did the United States grow as a result of the war with Mexico?

Canada Achieves Self-Rule

8. Analyze Sequence As you read "Canada Achieves Self-Rule," examine the text for the order of events. Then use a chart like this one to record major events that led to Canada's independence.

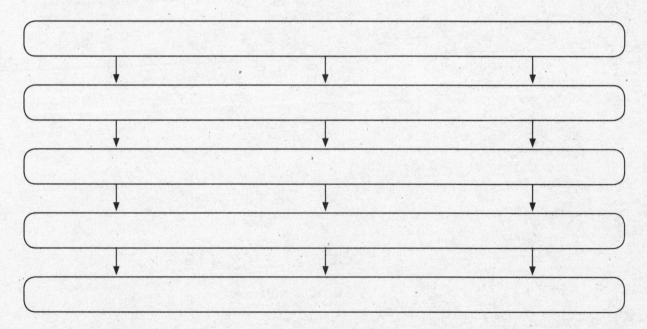

PRIMARY SOURCE EXPLORATION

Varied Responses to Western Imperialism

Introduction

Imperialism seemed like an unstoppable force by the late 1800s. Industrial powers set up colonies in some regions and exerted economic and military control in others. The people in these regions responded in a variety of ways, ranging from resistance to cooperation. A few nations, such as Siam and Ethiopia, managed to retain their independence. And one turned itself into an imperial power.

Document-Based Writing Activity

Analyze the following four sources and then use information from the documents and your knowledge of world history to write an essay in which you

- Describe the ways people in different lands responded to imperialism.
- Discuss which responses you think were most likely to be effective.

Keep in mind that your essay should include an introduction, several paragraphs, and a conclusion. In the body of the essay, use evidence from at least three documents. Support your response with relevant facts, examples, and details. In developing your essay, be sure to keep these general definitions in mind:

- *Describe* means "to illustrate something in words or tell about it."
- *Discuss* means "to make observations about something using facts, reasoning, and argument; to present in some detail."

Source 1

The War of the Golden Stool, 1900

In the late 1800s, the British in the Gold Coast colony of West Africa (now Ghana) fought a series of wars against the Ashanti kingdom. The last began when the British governor demanded that he be given the Ashanti throne known as the Golden Stool. In response, Ashanti queen Yaa Asantewaa called for war. The two speeches here are among several surviving versions of the only Ashanti account.

Governor Frederick Hodgson

Your king Prempeh I is in exile and will not return to Ashanti. His power and authority will be taken over by the Representative of the Queen of Britain. The terms of the 1874 Peace Treaty of Fomena, which required you to pay the cost of the 1874 war, have not been forgotten. You have to pay with interest the sum of £160,000 a year. Then there is the matter of the Golden Stool of Ashanti. The Queen is entitled to the stool; she must receive it. Where is the Golden Stool? … However, you may be quite sure that though the government has not received the Golden Stool at his hands it will rule over you with the same impartiality and fairness as if you had produced it.

Queen Yaa Asantewaa

Now I have seen that some of you fear to go forward to fight for our King. If it were in the brave days of old, the days of Osei Tutu, Okomfo Anokye, and Opolu Ware, chiefs would not sit down to see their King taken away without firing a shot. No white man could have dared to speak to chiefs of the Ashanti in the way the Governor spoke to you chiefs this morning. Is it true that the bravery of the Ashanti is no more? I cannot believe it. Yea, it cannot be! I must say this: if you the men of Ashanti will not go forward, then we will. We the women will. I shall call upon my fellow women. We will fight the white men. We will fight till the last of us falls in the battlefields!

---

1. What attitude toward the Ashanti does Hodgson display in his speech?

2. Who was the audience for Yaa Asantewaa's speech? What was her purpose?

3. Why was the Golden Stool important to both sides in this conflict?

Source 2

The Invasion of Mexico: Proclamation of President Juárez, 1862

In July 1861, Mexican president Benito Juárez announced that Mexico would suspend interest payments on French, British, and Spanish loans for two years. The three European powers responded by sending troops to Mexico. Britain and Spain soon withdrew when they realized France intended to conquer all of Mexico. Here, Juárez responds to the invasion.

MEXICANS: The warnings of the approaching war which was preparing in Europe against us have begun, unfortunately, to be realized. Spanish forces have invaded our territory; our national dignity is insulted; and perhaps, independence in danger....

All nations, and more especially Spain, have passed through times of penury and want, and almost all have had creditors who have waited for better times in which to secure themselves. From Mexico alone are sacrifices beyond her strength required. If the Spanish nation cloak other designs under the financial question, and with the pretext of groundless insults, her intentions shall soon be known. But the Government which must prepare the country for any event, proclaims, as the basis of its policy, that it does not declare war, but will repel force by force as far as its means will permit. That it is disposed to satisfy the claims against it founded on equity and justice, but without accepting conditions which cannot be admitted without offending the dignity of the nation or compromising its independence.

Mexicans, if such upright intentions be despised, if it be intended to humiliate Mexico, to dismember her territory, to interfere in her internal policy and Government, or perhaps extinguish her nationality, I appeal to your patriotism, and urge you that, laying aside the hatreds and enmities to which the diversity of our opinions has given rise, and sacrificing your properties and your blood, you rally united around the Government, and in defense of a cause the greatest and most sacred among men -- the defense of our country! Exaggerated and sinister reports from the enemies of Mexico have presented us before the world as uncivilized and degraded. Let us defend ourselves in the war to which we are provoked, observing strictly the laws and usages established for the sake of humanity. Let the defenseless enemy live in peace and security under the protection of our laws. Then shall we repel the calumnies [lies] of our enemies, and prove ourselves worthy of the liberty and independence bequeathed us by our fathers.

1. How does Juárez view the demands that Mexico pay its debts?

2. What appeal does he make to Mexican people of all classes?

3. Why do you think Juárez focuses on Spain even though France proved to be the greater threat?

Source 3

Rahimatulla M. Sayani, Presidential Address to the Twelfth Session of the Indian National Congress, 1896

Rahimatulla M. Sayani was one of two Indian Muslims present at the first meeting of the Indian National Congress in 1885. He later served as its president. The INC represented the educated elite of British-ruled India. In later years, it would come to demand complete independence. Here, Sayani outlines some of the early goals of the INC.

The following is a brief analysis of the declarations of the Congress leaders:

(a) To remember that we are all children of our mother-country, India, and that as such we are bound to love and respect each other and have common fellow-feeling for each other, and that each one of us should regard as his own the interests of the rest of us.

(b) That we should endeavour to promote personal intimacy and friendship amongst all the great communities of India, to develop and consolidate sentiments of national growth and unity, to weld them together into one nationality, to effect a moral union amongst them, to remove the taunt that we are not a nation, but only a [collection] of races and creeds which have no cohesion in them, and to bring about stronger and stronger friendly ties of common nationality….

(d) That we should work together for our common elevation; that we should work in the spirit that we are Indians and owe a duty to our country and to all our countrymen; that we should all work with a singleness of purpose for the amelioration of our country….

(h) That we should remember that right and truth must ever prevail in the end; that it is not by violence or by noise that great things are achieved, nor by ambition or self-seeking; that it is by calm, indomitable reliance on that moral force, which is the supreme reason, that a nation's life can be regenerated; that we should avoid taking jumps into the unknown.

(i) That the best interests of the Indian taxpayer lie in peace, economy, and reform; that his motto should be peace, loyalty, and progress. That the first, most essential requisite for his happiness is the assurance of permanent peace and the rigid maintenance of law and order.

(j) That our business is to represent to Government our reasonable grievances and our political disabilities and aspirations.

---

1. How does this document support the idea that the INC was a nationalist group?

2. How does this document indicate some of the internal problems India faced?

3. According to Sayani, how does the INC approach its relationship to the British government in India?

Source 4

Images of the Modernization and Westernization of Japan

Japan's response to western imperialism differed from that of other nations. These images illustrate the path that Japan took after Commodore Perry of the United States forced Japan to open itself to foreign trade and influence.

This 1875 print from a London newspaper was captioned "Progress of Civilisation in Japan."

Japanese women work in one of the many factories built as a result of the Meiji Restoration.

1. What does the picture on the left indicate about life in Japan after the Meiji Restoration?

2. How does the caption of the picture demonstrate bias?

3. How does the photograph at the right show that Japan followed Western industrial models?

Lesson 1 World War I Begins

CLOSE READING

European Powers Form Alliances

1. **Compare and Contrast** Read the two quotes from the text below.

   What evidence supports each man's viewpoint?

   > **"The future belongs to peace."**
   > —French economist Frédéric Passy

   > **"I shall not live to see the Great War, but you will see it, and it will start in the east."**
   > —German Chancellor Otto von Bismarck

2. **Cite Evidence** Why did the countries of Europe believe that alliances would guarantee peace? Use evidence from the text in your answer.

Major Causes of World War I

3. **Vocabulary: Determine Meaning** Using context clues, determine the meaning of the term *arms race*.

4. **Identify Cause and Effect** How did imperialism lead to increased tension and stronger alliances?

The Balkan Powder Keg Explodes

5. **Synthesize** Why did Austria-Hungary and Germany go to war against Serbia? Think about and include elements of nationalism, international rivalries, and militarism in your answer.

The Alliance System Leads to War

6. **Analyze Sequence** Use the graphic organizer below to create a timeline. Fill in each box with the date that various nations went to war with each other. Then draw lines from each box to the correct point on the timeline. Start your timeline with the assassination of Archduke Francis Ferdinand. What conclusions can you draw from this timeline?

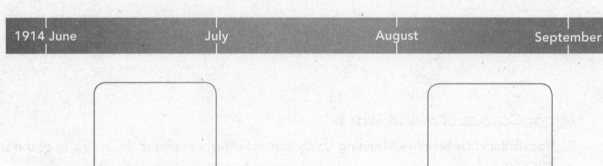

7. **Use Visual Information** Look at the map of European alliances in the text. Why did Germany fear an alliance between France and Russia?

Lesson 2 Fighting the Great War

CLOSE READING

A New Kind of War

1. **Analyze Style and Rhetoric** Reread the quote from the text below. Why do you think Schmieder contrasted the noise of war with birdsong? What does the passage tell us about the people who fought the war?

> "The blue French cloth mingled with the German grey upon the ground, and in some places the bodies were piled so high that one could take cover from shell-fire behind them. The noise was so terrific that orders had to be shouted by each man into the ear of the next. And whenever there was a momentary lull in the tumult of battle and the groans of the wounded, one heard, high up in the blue sky, the joyful song of birds! Birds singing just as they do at home in spring-time! It was enough to tear the heart out of one's body!"
>
> —German soldier Richard Schmieder writing from the trenches in France

Modern Military Technology

2. **Summarize** Using the concept web graphic organizer, summarize the key technologies used in the war and their effects.

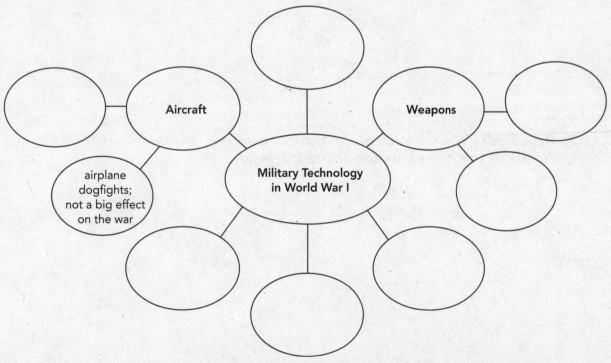

Other European Fronts

3. **Make Inferences** Why were there such high casualties on the Eastern Front?

4. **Hypothesize** Did the battles in Italy and the Balkans have an impact on the outcome of the war? Why or why not?

A Global Conflict

5. **Use Visual Information** Using the map in this lesson for reference, describe why the Dardanelles were important and what happened there.

6. **Summarize** What happened to Turkish Armenians during World War I?

7. **Hypothesize** Why did some people from the European colonies think that fighting in World War I might lead to citizenship or independence?

Lesson 3 World War I Ends

CLOSE READING

Governments Direct Total War

1. **Compare and Contrast** Read the two paragraphs under the heading "Blockades and Submarines Impact Economies." How did both Britain and Germany violate international law?

2. **Cite Evidence** In what ways did women's contributions and experiences during World War I directly contribute to social and political changes for women after the war?

Morale Breaks Down

3. **Identify Cause and Effect** What impact did the Russian Revolution have on the Allied war effort in Europe?

The United States Enters the War

4. **Draw Conclusions** President Wilson described World War I as a "war to end war." What efforts did he make to deliver on that promise?

The Great War Ends

5. **Analyze Interactions Among Events** Uprisings by hungry people in cities across Germany contributed to Kaiser William's decision to step down in September 1918. What events together caused widespread hunger in Germany?

6. **Analyze Data** Using data in the infographic "The Costs of World War I," describe how American financial costs and casualties compared to the costs and casualties borne by the other Allies. How can you explain these differences?

Making the Peace

7. **Determine Effects** In what ways was Germany forced to make amends for the outbreak of World War I?

Effects of the Peace Settlements

8. **Integrate Information from Diverse Sources** Read the fifth of Wilson's Fourteen Points. Then read the two paragraphs in the section "The Mandate System." Do you think the Allies followed Wilson's recommendation for dealing with colonial holdings? Why or why not?

Lesson 4 Revolution in Russia

CLOSE READING

Causes of the February Revolution

1. **Identify Cause and Effect** How was World War I a major cause of revolution in Russia? Provide specific details from the text to support your answer.

2. **Analyze Interactions Among Ideas** According to Marxism, the proletariat would overthrow governments and set up a classless society in which wealth and power would be equally shared. Did Lenin's version of Marxism remain true to the spirit of Marxism? Why or why not?

Lenin Leads the Bolsheviks

3. **Identify Cause and Effect** How did the Bolsheviks gain power and momentum?

The October Revolution Brings the Bolsheviks to Power

4. **Identify Cause and Effect** How did the actions and inactions of the Russian provisional government cause the October Revolution?

5. **Draw Conclusions** Why was Lenin's promise of "Peace, Land, and Bread" so effective in gaining support for the Bolsheviks? Did Lenin fulfill his promise to the Russian people? Cite evidence from the text to support your answer.

Civil War Erupts in Russia

6. **Analyze Interactions** How were the Reds able to defeat the Whites in the Russian Civil War?

The Communist Soviet Union Emerges

7. **Assess an Argument** The Communists drew up a constitution that, according to the text, asserted that "all political power, resources, and means of production would belong to workers and peasants." How truthful was this assertion? How do you think this affected the credibility of the Soviet Union?

PRIMARY SOURCE EXPLORATION

Impact of War Beyond the Battlefield

Introduction

In 1914, an assassination set events in motion that sparked World War I, a global outbreak of conflict that brought death and suffering on a scale never before seen. The impact of the war reached far beyond the battlefield, affecting soldiers and civilians alike. The experience of soldiers, particularly British soldiers on the Western Front, was captured by letters, diaries, memoirs and works of literature and art. But the war affected nearly all members of society in one way or another beyond the battlefield.

Document-Based Writing Activity

Analyze the following five sources and then use information from the documents and your knowledge of world history to write an essay in which you

- Describe how the war impacted women and children on the home front.
- Discuss how the war affected minority ethnic and religious groups and colonial populations.

Keep in mind that your essay should include an introduction, several paragraphs, and a conclusion. In the body of the essay, use evidence from at least three documents. Support your response with relevant facts, examples, and details. In developing your essay, be sure to keep these general definitions in mind:

- *Describe* means "to illustrate something in words or tell about it."
- *Discuss* means "to make observations about something using facts, reasoning, and argument; to present in some detail."

Source 1

Accounts of military recruitment in the French colony of Senegal during World War I, from Memoirs of the Maelstrom, Joe Lunn, 1999

In 1914, France and Britain both controlled large parts of Africa as colonies, with other European countries (including Germany) controlling smaller parts of the huge continent. France required its colonies to provide soldiers, often called *tirailleurs sénégalais* (regardless of whether or not they were from the Senegalese part of their French West Africa colony). Some colonial soldiers joined willingly; others were coerced.

Biram Mbodji Tine: "Many of the young men fled from the village [when the chef de canton came to take soldiers]. [But] they used to arrest their fathers [if] they [did not] come back. [And] often their mothers used to say to their sons [when they returned from the countryside for food]: "You know that your name has been written [down by the chef de canton] and [yet] you ran away. And now your father has been arrested and he will be taken [to] prison. So go and enter the army." And often they used to go and enter the army [so that] their fathers [would be] released."

Sera Ndiaye: "In each family they only took one young man, never two. And my father decided that I should go and enter the army instead of my elder brother. Because, he told me, "If I die, your elder brother could care for the family, but you are too young for that." That's why he sent me into the army. I was not happy to go, [but] because I was very close to my father . . . I felt obliged to."

Coumba Kebe: "Many, many young men used to run away [whenever the recruiting "agents" were seen near the village]. [And] when they ran, they used to go to a [Mandinka] village called Wai—it was [in Guinea-Bissau]. And whenever you crossed the frontier, no one was allowed to touch you....... And on the road to this village, there was a bridge. And eventually, the bridge broke down because of the [number] of men that were crossing over it."

Souan Gor Diatta: "When the Tubabs [Europeans] first came [to recruit soldiers], there was resistance. But the people of the village only had very old rifles—you had to put powder in them and a ball—"muskets." But they took their muskets to fight with the Tubabs. But when they began to fight—when [the soldiers opened fire and] they saw that the Tubabs had very modern rifles—they decided to run away. But some of them were killed before they ran."

1. According to the accounts of Tine, Ndiaye, and Diatta, what techniques did the French use to get Senegalese men to enlist in the French military?

2. Why would some Senegalese men choose to resist being recruited?

3. What do these accounts reveal about the attitude of people subjected to colonial rule?

Source 2

"R.H. Davis Tells of Louvain Horrors," Richard Harding Davis, New York Tribune, August 31, 1914

American reporter Richard Harding Davis rushed to Belgium when war broke out and wrote several articles about what he witnessed there during the German invasion. He believed that the United States should intervene on the side of the Allies.

War on the Defenceless

. . . In other wars I have watched men on one hilltop, without haste, without heat, fire at men on another hill, and in consequence on both sides good men were wasted. But in those fights there were no women or children, and the shells struck only vacant stretches of veldt [open country] or uninhabited mountainsides.

At Louvain [a city in Belgium] it was war upon the defenceless, war upon churches, colleges, shops of milliners and lacemakers; war brought to the bedside and the fireside; against children in wooden shoes at play in the streets. . . .

Men to Be Shot Marched Past

You could tell when an officer passed by the electric torch he carried strapped to the chest. In the darkness the gray uniforms filled the station with an army of ghosts. You distinguished men only when pipes hanging from their teeth glowed red or their bayonets flashed.

Outside the station in the public square the people of Louvain passed in an unending procession, women bareheaded, weeping, men carrying the children asleep on their shoulders, all hemmed in by the shadowy army of gray wolves. Once they were halted, and among them were marched a line of men. They well knew their fellow townsmen. These were on their way to be shot. And better to point the moral an officer halted both processions and, climbing to a cart, explained why the men were to die. He warned others not to bring down upon themselves a like vengeance.

As those being led to spend the night in the fields looked across to those marked for death they saw old friends, neighbors of long standing, men of their own household. The officer bellowing at them from the cart was illuminated by the headlights of an automobile. He looked like an actor held in a spotlight on a darkened stage.

1. According to this account, how did the tactics of warfare change during World War I?

2. Why do you think the invaders used these tactics?

3. Who was the audience of this article and what effect would reading it have on its readers?

Source 3

Speech at London Polytechnic, Emmeline Pankhurst, June 24, 1915

Emmeline Pankhurst, with her daughter Christabel, was a leader in the British women's suffragist movement. She was arrested more than a dozen times as a result of various protests. When Britain declared war in 1914, she suspended her suffragist campaign and focused instead on how women could help the war effort.

Women are eating their hearts out with desire to see their services utilised in this national emergency. It is not a question with us of war bonuses; it is not a question of red tape, which has to be slowly untied. With us it is not a question of these things; but we realise that if the war is to be won, the whole energy of the nation and the whole capacity of the nation will have to be utilised in order to win. . . .

How is it that men can be so behind as not to see that the fire of patriotism burns in the hearts of women quite as strongly as it does in the hearts of men[?]. . . .

I am one of those people who, at the right time and in the proper place, are prepared to fight for certain ideals of freedom and liberty and would be willing to give my life for them; we are prepared to hold great organising meetings all over the country and enlist women for war service if they will only set us free to do it. We here and now this afternoon offer our services to the Government, to recruit and enlist the women of the country for war service, whether that war service is the making of munitions or whether that war service is the replacing of skilled men who have been called up, so that the business of the country can go on.

1. What does this excerpt suggest about women's stance on fighting the Great War?

2. Why would this attitude be surprising to some people at the time?

3. How is this perspective reflected in warfare today?

Source 4

Account of Jewish Persecution, S. Ansky, Published in The Enemy at His Pleasure, *Joachim Neugroschel, 2003*

During World War I, prejudice and resentment aimed at ethnic minorities took a deadly turn, with the loyalties of ethnic minorities called into question. A Jewish Russian reporter talked to Jews living in Lodz, now in Poland but then part of the Russian Empire, about their experiences.

"Of all the ordeals we've suffered in Lodz," he told me, "the worst was the way the Poles treated us. There was no lie they wouldn't spread about us. When airplanes were flying overhead, one man standing out on his porch looked up and sneezed. The Poles reported him, claiming that his sneeze was a signal indicating where to drop the bombs, even though the planes were high up, and the man was arrested. Another time, the Poles dragged a Jew to headquarters and accused him of hiding a German pilot. A plane had crashed near the man's house and the pilot had vanished. Maybe the Jew had concealed him. And even though he argued that he hadn't even seen the plane, that the whole story was a fabrication, they jailed him. Next they went to get the fallen aircraft but they couldn't find it. And instead of concluding that the whole story was fantasy, they arrested two more Jews on suspicion of hiding the plane.

However the worst suffering came from the Sokols, the nationalistic Slavic organizations. When the Germans took Lodz a second time, the Sokols came with them and terrorized us. They forced young men to join them. We ran, we hid, and then resorted to the most persuasive kind of inducement: bribes. At first we paid them a hundred or just fifty rubles apiece. Later on, a three-kopek coin was enough. In the end, when the Germans pulled out and the Russians returned to Lodz, the Poles circulated a rumor that the Sokols were really Jewish groups in disguise. They actually called them Jewish brigades."

1. What does this excerpt describe, and what was its cause?

2. What other groups experienced this treatment during World War I?

3. Why might this type of behavior recur in subsequent wars?

Source 5

Images of Aerial Bombardment

Airplane technology was in its infancy during World War I, but airplanes were still used to observe troop movements and to help direct artillery fire, punctuated by some spectacular aerial dogfights. In some cases, planes or zeppelins were used to drop bombs on enemy troops and civilians—a tactic that would be used much more heavily during World War II.

Officials in Yarmouth, England, sift through the rubble of a building destroyed in an air raid.

Allied bombers target German bases in occupied Belgium.

1. What do these two photos depict?

2. How would these events affect morale on the home front as well as on the battlefield?

3. In what ways did technologies such as this permanently change the impact of war?

Lesson 1 Revolution and Nationalism in Latin America

CLOSE READING

The Mexican Revolution

1. **Identify Cause and Effect** Describe at least three reasons people supported the Mexican Revolution.

2. **Infer** Why was dictator Porfirio Díaz elected president so many times? What finally made people turn against him and demand changes to the government?

3. **Identify Cause and Effect** Why did Victoriano Huerta and other rebels force Francisco Madero to resign?

4. **Draw Conclusions** Why did Venustiano Carranza turn on his allies Emiliano Zapata and Francisco "Pancho" Villa?

Economic and Social Reform

5. **Summarize** What were the main provisions of the Mexican Constitution of 1917?

6. Draw Conclusions Why was land distribution such a key issue in Mexico?

Nationalism Spreads in Latin America

7. Identify Cause and Effect How did the Great Depression affect Latin America?

8. Analyze Interactions How did Latin American writers, artists, and thinkers react to events during the 1920s?

9. Identify Central Issues In what ways did Franklin Roosevelt change the policy of the United States toward Latin America? Provide examples from the text.

Lesson 2 Nationalist Movements in Africa and the Middle East

CLOSE READING

Africans Protest Colonial Rule

1. **Summarize** How did the European governments treat Black Africans in Kenya and Rhodesia? Why did the governments act this way? Cite evidence from the text.

2. **Identify Cause and Effect** What role did the ANC play in South Africa? What was the effect of its actions?

A Rising Tide of African Nationalism

3. **Identify Cause and Effect** What was the Pan-African Congress? How effective was it? Explain.

4. **Draw Conclusions** How did some writers in West Africa and the Caribbean create a sense of pride among Africans? How might their work have affected readers outside Africa?

5. **Identify Supporting Details** Why did the British government grant Egypt independence in 1922?

Modernization of Turkey and Persia

6. **Compare** Complete the graphic organizer to compare the rule of Atatürk and Reza Khan.

Leader/Nation	Business/Economy	Law/Government	Society
Reza Khan/ Persia (Iran)			
Atatürk/Turkey			

7. **Identify Cause and Effect** Why did a nationalist movement grow in Persia after World War I?

Nationalism and Conflict in the Middle East

8. **Identify Cause and Effect** Why did foreign companies begin to move to the Middle East after World War I? How did Arab nationalists respond?

9. **Synthesize** What promise did the Allies make to Arabs in the Palestine Mandate? How did it conflict with the Balfour Declaration? What was the result of these actions? Cite evidence from the text.

260   **Close Reading** ▪ The World Between the Wars

Lesson 3 India Seeks Self-Rule

CLOSE READING

India's Struggle for Independence Begins

1. **Identify Supporting Details** How was Gandhi treated when he returned to India? Why?

2. **Analyze Sequence** Complete the graphic organizer to show how World War I started a chain of events that led to the Congress party's call for independence.

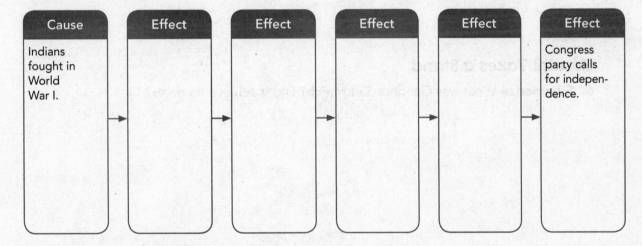

Cause	Effect	Effect	Effect	Effect	Effect
Indians fought in World War I.					Congress party calls for independence.

3. **Identify Cause and Effect** What were the Rowlatt Acts? What effect did they have on the nationalist movement?

Gandhi's Philosophy of Civil Disobedience

4. Summarize Summarize Gandhi's main beliefs.

5. Check Understanding How did Gandhi apply Henry David Thoreau's idea about civil disobedience to India's political situation?

Gandhi Takes a Stand

6. Summarize What was Gandhi's Salt March? Did it achieve its goals?

7. Evaluate Explanations What reasons did the British government give for postponing independence during the late 1930s? What was the effect of this decision?

Lesson 4 New Forces in China and Japan

CLOSE READING

Trouble in the Chinese Republic

1. **Identify Causes** As you read "Trouble in the Chinese Republic," complete the following chart by listing the multiple causes of upheaval in the Chinese republic.

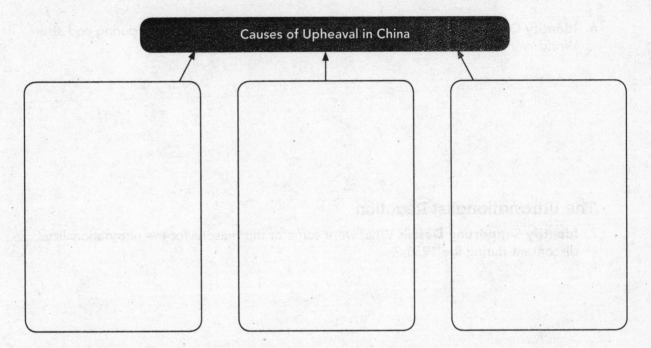

Causes of Upheaval in China

2. **Identify Cause and Effect** What were two responses of the Chinese people to the country's problems?

Nationalists and Communists

3. **Identify Cause and Effect** How did the Long March contribute to the rise of communism in China?

China Faces Japanese Imperialism

4. **Contrast** Marxism was based on the rise of the proletariat, or industrial working class. How was Chinese communism different from classic Marxism?

Conflicting Forces in Japan

5. Cite Evidence What were some sources of unrest in Japan during the 1920s?

6. Identify Central Issues Why did Japan want to expand its territories during and after World War I?

The Ultranationalist Reaction

7. Identify Supporting Details What were some of the reasons for the ultranationalists' discontent during the 1930s?

Militarists Gain Power

8. Infer Why did militarists and ultranationalists glorify Hirohito and encourage the revival of traditional values?

9. Generate Explanations How did the government react to the demands of the ultranationalists?

Lesson 5 The West After World War I

CLOSE READING

Social Change After World War I

1. **Identify Supporting Details** As you read the sections "Social Changes After World War I," "Scientific Discoveries," "Literature Reflects New Perspectives," and "Modern Art and Architecture" in your textbook, complete the concept web below to identify supporting details.

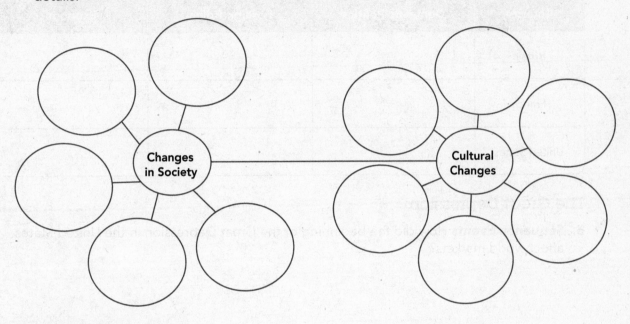

Scientific Discoveries

2. **Summarize** Why did Curie's and Einstein's theories unsettle the general public?

Literature Reflects New Perspectives
Modern Art and Architecture

3. **Compare** What did surrealism have in common with the stream-of-consciousness technique and Freud's work?

Postwar Politics in the West and International Relations and Economics in the Postwar Era

4. Identify Main Ideas As you read "Postwar Politics in the West," "International Relations," and "Economics in the Postwar Era," complete the chart below to identify the main ideas under each heading. Use each row to record information for a different country.

Postwar Issues			
Country	**Domestic Politics**	**Foreign Policy**	**Economics**
Britain			
France			
United States			

The Great Depression

5. Sequence Events How did the beginning of the Great Depression in the United States affect world markets?

Western Democracies React to the Depression

6. Evaluate Arguments Was the New Deal successful? Explain.

Lesson 6 Fascism Emerges in Italy

CLOSE READING

The Rise of Mussolini

1. **Identify Main Ideas** As you read "The Rise of Mussolini" and "Mussolini's Totalitarian Rule," complete the flow chart below by identifying the main ideas and events under each heading.

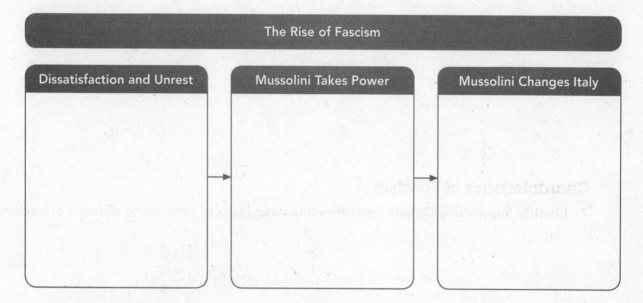

The Rise of Fascism

| Dissatisfaction and Unrest | Mussolini Takes Power | Mussolini Changes Italy |

2. **Identify Central Issues** What were postwar conditions like in Italy?

3. **Generate Explanations** Explain why you think people found Mussolini appealing.

Mussolini's Totalitarian Rule

4. **Make Generalizations** What was Fascist policy regarding children?

5. **Support Ideas with Examples** What were some of the ways Mussolini won political support?

6. **Summarize** Describe the Italian economy under Mussolini.

Characteristics of Fascism

7. **Identify Supporting Details** Describe some basic features common to all forms of fascism.

8. **Analyze Interactions** How did Fascists view democracy?

9. **Sequence Events** How did the reaction of the West to Mussolini's government change over time?

Lesson 7 The Soviet Union Under Stalin

CLOSE READING

Stalin Builds a Command Economy

1. Identify Central Ideas What are some of the differences between a command economy and a capitalist economy?

2. Generate Explanations Why did some peasants resist the collectivization plan? How did Stalin respond to the peasant resistance of collectivization?

Control Through Terror

3. Summarize What was the Great Purge? How did the purges increase Stalin's power?

4. Draw Conclusions How do you think Stalin's policies of terror affected the people of the Soviet Union and their feelings toward their government?

Stalin Builds a Totalitarian State

5. Support Ideas with Evidence Describe some of the ways Stalin controlled cultural life in the Soviet Union.

6. **Summarize** How did the treatment of artists and writers change under Stalin's rule?

Soviet Society Under Stalin

7. **Draw Conclusions** Who do you think made up the elite in Soviet society? How were these people treated differently from the rest of the Russian population?

8. **Identify Main Ideas** Why were state-run schools important to Stalin's communist goals?

Soviet Foreign Policy

9. **Draw Conclusions** Why were Western nations wary of the Comintern?

10. **Compare** Describe the similarities in the foreign policy goals of Lenin and Stalin.

Lesson 8 The Rise of Nazi Germany

CLOSE READING

The Weimar Republic

1. **Draw Conclusions** Which factor do you think might have been most significant in Hitler's rise to power? Explain your answer.

2. **Infer** Why do you think culture flourished in the Weimar Republic despite the government's problems?

Hitler Leads the Nazi Party

3. **Determine Central Ideas** How did Hitler shift political thought in Weimar Germany? Why did his radical ideas gain the support of many Germans?

4. **Explain an Argument** Explain Nazi ideology as depicted in Hitler's book *Mein Kampf*.

The Third Reich

5. Analyze Interactions How did Hitler expand his control over the German people?

6. Summarize How did Hitler's anti-Semitism increase over time?

Authoritarian Rule in Eastern Europe

7. Compare Identify two ways that dictators from other Eastern European countries were similar to Hitler.

8. Infer How did World War I impact the rise of authoritarian rule in Eastern Europe?

PRIMARY SOURCE EXPLORATION

The Struggle for Women's Suffrage

Introduction

As male suffrage expanded, women began to demand equal rights. In Great Britain, Mary Wollenstonecraft is given credit for starting the movement with the publication of *A Vindication of the Rights of Woman* in 1792. The demand for women's suffrage increased once the matter was taken up by John Stuart Mill and his wife in the 1850s. But for many years, suffrage legislation was defeated. Voting rights for women in Great Britain were granted in 1918. An international movement for equal voting rights intensified. Most countries granted voting rights to women during the early and mid-twentieth century.

Document-Based Writing Activity

Analyze the following four sources and then use information from the documents and your knowledge of world history to write an essay in which you

- Describe how women worked to gain voting privileges.
- Discuss the results of the struggle. Were women successful? Did gaining suffrage change society?

Keep in mind that your essay should include an introduction, several paragraphs, and a conclusion. In the body of the essay, use evidence from at least three documents. Support your response with relevant facts, examples, and details. In developing your essay, be sure to keep these general definitions in mind:

- *Describe* means "to illustrate something in words or tell about it."
- *Discuss* means "to make observations about something using facts, reasoning, and argument; to present in some detail."

Source 1

An Appeal to the Men of New Zealand by Mary Müller, 1869

The feminist movement took a strong hold in New Zealand at the end of the nineteenth century. The struggle was part of an ongoing international effort to change the status of women in society. In New Zealand, the call for granting women the right to vote was widely supported. Eventually, New Zealand would become the first country in the world to grant women the right to vote. But, before that, a long struggle took place.

A wise ancient declared that the most perfect popular government was "where an injury done to the meanest subject is an insult upon the whole constitution". What. . .can be said for a Government that deliberately inflicts injury upon a great mass of its intelligent and respectable subjects; that virtually ignores their existence. . . Custom use; it has always been so. This may be enough to say of the past. . .but is it to be remedied [improved] for the future? How long are women to remain a wholly unrepresented body of the people? This is a question that has of late been agitated [argued about] in England, and women in this colony read, watch, and reflect. Though their household cares chiefly occupy them, yet many find leisure in the quiet evening hours to read not only their fashions, and [the] colonial [papers] but the English papers also. They cannot remain ignorant of the agitation of this, to them great matter, and it has struck the writer of these few pages that I might be wholly vain to make an appeal to the men of this our adopted land.

Mark the sudden questions of a bright eager girl, or the quiet remark of some sensible matron, upon a political matter in the newspaper before her, and see the cold stare of surprise, or hear the rebuke [criticism] about women seeking to step beyond their province, . . . and can you marvel that the girl turns to gossip about the new fashions, or the mother takes refuge in discussions upon servants, sewing machines, and other minor domestic details? Women of the middle class suffer most from this open, systematic putting down. . .

1. According to the author, what great injury has the government inflicted upon the population?

2. What is the reaction of women in New Zealand to the suffrage movement in England? Why do you think the author points this out?

3. Why do you think the author devotes most of her argument to defending the intelligence of women?

Source 2

A Timeline of Women's Suffrage Granted by Countries

The chart below shows when women were granted the right to vote in some countries.

Country	Year Women Gained the Vote
New Zealand	1893
Australia	1902 (Indigenous Australian women could vote in 1962)
Finland	1906
Norway	1913
Canada	1916 (By 1960, Asian-Canadian and First-Nation women could vote)
Austria, Germany, Poland, Russia	1918
Netherlands	1919
United States	1920
Sweden	1921
Spain	1931
Turkey	1924
France	1944
Italy	1945
Argentina, Japan, Mexico, Pakistan	1947
China	1949
India	1950
Colombia	1954
Egypt	1956
Algeria	1962
Switzerland	1971
Bangladesh	1972
Jordan	1974
Portugal	1976
South Africa	1994
Kuwait	2005
United Arab Emirates	2006
Saudi Arabia	2011

1. What does this chart show about the duration of the struggle?

2. What countries took longer to grant equal voting rights to all women?

Source 3

Suffrage Fallacies, Mrs. A.J. George, 1916

The cause for women's suffrage was not welcomed by all women. Opposition to the cause existed. In the late nineteenth and early twentieth century, female anti-suffragists protested the "burden of the ballot." Alice George presents her anti-suffrage argument.

Woman suffrage must ultimately fail. It is based upon a fallacy, [false reasoning] and no fallacy has ever made a permanent conquest over mankind.

"The history of mankind," declared the founders of the suffrage movement, "is a history of repeated injuries. . .on the part of man toward woman. . ."

On this false foundation was built the votes for women temple. How shall it endure? . . In a healthy state of society there is no rivalry between men and women, they were created different, and in the economy of life have different duties, but their interests are the common interests of humanity. . . .the women of every social group are represented in a well-ordered government, automatically and inevitably, by the men of the group.

Thus far, we have made a few crude experiments in double suffrage, but nowhere has equal suffrage been tried. Equal suffrage implies a fair field with favor to none- a field where woman, stripped of legal and civil advantages, must take her place as man's rival in the struggle for existence, for, in the long run, women cannot have equal rights and retain special privileges. If the average woman is to be a voter she must accept jury service and aid in the protection of life and property.

No question of superiority or equality is involved in the opposition to votes for women. The test of women's worth is her ability to solve the problems and do the work she must face as a woman if the race is not to deteriorate and civilization perish.

Anti-suffragists contend that the average woman can serve best by remaining a non-partisan and working for the common good outside the realms of political strife. To prove this contention [argument] they point to what women have done without the ballot and what they have failed to do with it.

1. How does George respond to the suffragist argument that men do not treat women as equals?

2. What responsibilities, according to George, must women be willing to accept if they gained the right to vote?

3. How does George support her argument that women do not need the vote to change society?

Source 4

A Long Road to Women's Suffrage in Saudi Arabia, by Elizabeth Dickinson, 2015

In 2011, King Abdullah of Saudi Arabia declared that the women of Saudi Arabia would be allowed to vote for local councils that had been formed in 2005. The election would not occur until 2015. The article below describes the women's experience under this new law.

When voter registration opened in August, few of Rana's friends noticed, and the 25-year old recent college graduate drew curious looks when she brought it up. None of them were planning to participate in Saudi Arabia's December 12 municipal elections—the first vote in which women will be allowed to stand as voters and candidates. "My friends know about the election, but they are not excited about it," she recalled on an October afternoon from her office in a Jeddah PR company. "They didn't register [to vote]." Rana had felt differently. Sure, it was a small step, and maybe little would come of it. But she was insistent, "We need women to get into this process," she told her friends and family—and herself. "Women can do things for society."

But in Rana's case, those things don't include registering to vote. Rana ticked off the many obstacles she encountered. The window for registration was too brief, the documentation required too onerous, and her legal guardian—which all Saudi women require for even the most basic bureaucratic chores—wasn't around to arrange her paperwork. And her family, inclined to think of politics as a man's domain, discouraged her efforts. Across Saudi Arabia, Rana's experience was shared by countless peers.

Saudi policymakers and female activists alike touted the monarchy's introduction of universal suffrage in municipal elections as a landmark in relaxing the country's notoriously strict constraints on women. (Females in Saudi Arabia are treated as legal dependents from birth to death and can make few decisions—from travel to schooling—without a man's consent.) But the disappointing registration numbers seem to tell another story. Some naysayers are already arguing that it proves women aren't capable or interested in being involved in politics. Yet low registration numbers are less a reflection of female interest than an indication of just how many barriers still stand in the way of Saudi women hoping to participate in public life. A registration process meant to empower women ended up being a reminder of the many ways female citizens are still held back.

It's not how many imagined universal suffrage unfolding back in 2011, when the late King Abdullah announced that women would be allowed to vote for the local councils that were first formed in 2005, and wield influence over whether projects like new roads and sewer systems are approved and how much they should cost. Authorities promised they would be ready for women to participate by 2015.

1. Why are there mixed feelings among the women about the upcoming election?

2. How effective are the voting rights granted to the women in Saudi Arabia? Explain.

Lesson 1 Aggression, Appeasement, and War

CLOSE READING

A Pattern of Aggression

1. **Summarize** Use the table below to summarize the acts of aggression.

Acts of Aggression	
Japan	
Italy	
Germany	

2. **Draw Inferences** How effective was the League of Nations combating aggression in 1930? Give details from the reading to support your answer.

3. **Determine Central Ideas** Why did Germany, Italy, and Japan reach an agreement to form the Axis Powers?

The Spanish Civil War

4. **Determine Central Ideas** How was the Spanish Civil War another step in the march towards World War II?

German Aggression Continues

5. **Sequence** Use the table below to sequence German acts of aggression.

German Aggression	
March 1938	
Sept 1938	
March 1939	
Sept 1939	

6. **Determine Central Ideas** Why did Britons and other people in Western Europe have mixed feelings about the Munich Agreement?

World War II Begins

7. **Draw Inferences** Why did the democracies finally promise to protect Poland from a German invasion?

8. **Determine Central Ideas** How did the Nazi-Soviet Pact influence Hitler's decision to invade Poland?

Lesson 2 Axis Powers Advance

CLOSE READING

Axis Domination of Europe

1. **Summarize** How did the Axis Powers achieve victories in 1939 and 1940?

2. **Infer** Why do you think airstrikes were important to Germany's plan to invade Britain?

3. **Identify Central Ideas** Explain the importance of Winston Churchill during World War II.

Nazis Attack the Soviet Union

4. **Identify Cause and Effect** How did Hitler's invasion of the Soviet Union affect the Nazi-Soviet Pact?

5. Draw Conclusions How did Hitler's invasion of the Soviet Union work against him?

U.S. Involvement in the War

6. Summarize Explain the sequence of events that led to U.S. entry into World War II.

7. Compare How was the Japanese attack on the U.S naval base at Pearl Harbor similar to the German invasion of Poland?

Lesson 3 The Holocaust

CLOSE READING

The Nazi Campaign Against the Jews

1. **Determine Central Ideas** How did the Nazis put their anti-Semitic beliefs into practice?

2. **Summarize** How did the Nazis use the concentration camp system throughout World War II?

3. **Contrast** How were death camps different from concentration camps? Which of Hitler's goals did the death camps address?

Jewish Resistance

4. **Determine Central Ideas** Why was it difficult for non-Jewish civilians to help, hide, or protect their Jewish neighbors?

5. **Draw Inferences** How were Warsaw Ghetto residents an inspiration to others?

The Allies Respond to the Holocaust

6. **Summarize** Why did the Allies take only limited action to protect the Jewish people in occupied Europe?

7. **Draw Inferences** After liberation, why was life difficult for European Jews who survived the Holocaust?

Lesson 4 The Allies Turn the Tide

CLOSE READING

A Commitment to Total War

1. **Integrate Information** Review the text concerning the Allies' war resources, and then look at the infographic showing the GDP for each country and the amount spent on certain resources for the war effort. Compare the two categories for each country. What do the text and the infographic show in terms of GDP of each country during the period 1939–1945 versus the Allied production of tanks and airplanes for the war effort?

2. **Summarize** How was business restructured on the Allied home fronts in order to support the war effort?

Progress on Three Fronts

3. **Draw Inferences** Why was Hitler's strategic decision to try to take over the oil fields of the Soviet Union a disaster? Use details from the text to support your answer.

4. **Summarize** Using the text, fill in the table below about the three main fronts of World War II during 1942 and 1943. List in each row the Allied and Axis leaders who were responsible for making the decisions on each front. Then, briefly list turning points on each of the fronts during the war.

	Leaders	Turning Point
Pacific		
North Africa and Italy		
Soviet Union		

A Second Front in Europe

5. **Identify Steps in a Process** In order to pave the way for the D-Day invasion, what preliminary steps did Eisenhower take to distract and weaken Germany?

6. **Identify Central Ideas** Using the visuals in the text and the narrative, provide a synopsis of what took place on the beaches of Normandy on D-Day and describe why it was so important for the Allies to succeed in this offensive.

Lesson 5 Victory for the Allies

CLOSE READING

End of the War in Europe

1. **Use Visual Information** Review the text and the photograph of the soldiers at the Elbe River. What is significant about shaking of hands by American and Soviet soldiers at this point in the war?

2. **Summarize** Hitler and Germany faced major challenges toward the end of the war. Using the graphic organizer below, fill in information about each fact or event that describes why it was a major challenge for Germany.

Fact or Event	Challenge
Battle of Stalingrad	
Germany's location	
U.S. military production	

Battles in the Pacific

3. **Paraphrase** Military operations in the Pacific theater were based on Allied collaboration, but operations were commanded by the U.S. Army, Navy, and Air Force. How did each contribute to Japan's defeat?

4. **Draw Inferences** Why was the victory at Guadalcanal a turning point in the war in the Pacific?

End of the War in the Pacific

5. Draw Conclusions Why was the United States interested in developing an atomic weapon?

6. Assess an Argument What were the general arguments for and against using atomic bombs to end World War II?

Aftermath of the War

7. Draw Inferences What financial costs do you think the Axis should have been responsible for, and why?

8. Identify Key Steps in a Process After winning World War II, the Allies wanted to ensure that Axis countries would not threaten peace once again. Make a list of steps the Allies took to guard against a rebirth of Axis aggression.

The United Nations Is Formed

9. Summarize What was the goal of the United Nations when it was created? How have its goals changed over time?

PRIMARY SOURCE EXPLORATION

Defeating the Nazis in Europe

Introduction

As World War II began, the Nazi war machine seemed unstoppable. And fighting against it required the cooperation of many nations. It also required the efforts of many people – soldiers and civilians, men and women, young and old. Some fought in battle, some worked behind enemy lines. But all contributed to the final defeat of Nazi Germany.

Document-Based Writing Activity

Analyze the following four sources and then use information from the documents and your knowledge of world history to write an essay in which you

- Describe the ways different individuals and groups contributed to the defeat of Germany.
- Evaluate the personal qualities needed to fight against the Nazis.

Keep in mind that your essay should include an introduction, several paragraphs, and a conclusion. In the body of the essay, use evidence from at least three documents. Support your response with relevant facts, examples, and details. In developing your essay, be sure to keep these general definitions in mind:

- *Describe* means "to illustrate something in words or tell about it."
- *Evaluate* means "to examine and judge the significance, worth, or condition of; to determine the value of."

Source 1

A pilot describes the Battle of Britain, in *Their Finest Hour, Michie and Grabner, 1941*

After the Nazi defeat of France, Britain stood alone against Germany. The Royal Air Force (RAF) defended the British Isles against attacks by the Nazi Luftwaffe. Here, RAF pilot John Beard – who was 21 at the time – describes his squadron's battle against German fighter planes in the skies over London.

It was really a terrific sight and quite beautiful. First they seemed just a cloud of light as the sun caught the many glistening chromium parts of their engines, their windshields, and the spin of their airscrew discs. Then, as our squadron hurtled nearer, the details stood out. I could see the bright-yellow noses of Messerschmitt fighters sandwiching the bombers, and could even pick out some of the types. The sky seemed full of them, packed in layers thousands of feet deep. They came on steadily, wavering up and down along the horizon. "Oh, golly," I thought, "golly, golly...."

And then any tension I had felt on the way suddenly left me. I was elated but very calm. I leaned over and switched on my reflector sight, flicked the catch on the gun button from 'Safe' to 'Fire,' and lowered my seat till the circle and dot on the reflector sight shone darkly red in front of my eyes....

Diving down, I noticed that the running progress of the battle had brought me over London again. I could see the network of streets with the green space of Kensington Gardens, and I had an instant's glimpse of the Round Pond, where I sailed boats when I was a child. In that moment, and as I was rapidly overhauling the Germans ahead, a Dornier 17 sped right across my line of flight, closely pursued by a Hurricane. And behind the Hurricane came two Messerschmitts. He was too intent to have seen them and they had not seen me! They were coming slightly toward me. It was perfect. A kick at the rudder and I swung in toward them, thumbed the gun button, and let them have it. The first burst was placed just the right distance ahead of the leading Messerschmitt. He ran slap into it and he simply came to pieces in the air. His companion, with one of the speediest and most brilliant 'get-outs' I have ever seen, went right away in a half Immelmann turn. I missed him completely. He must almost have been hit by the pieces of the leader but he got away. I hand it to him.

1. What evidence shows that Beard was a highly trained and skilled fighter pilot? Give two examples.

2. Why do you think Beard mentions looking down and seeing Round Pond?

3. What seems to be Beard's attitude toward the enemy planes and pilots?

Source 2

Interview with a member of the French resistance, David P. Boder, 1946

During the Nazi occupation of France, many French people collaborated with the Nazis. But others fought bravely against the occupiers. Women and men of the Resistance spread anti-Nazi propaganda, sabotaged German war efforts, even killed Nazi officers. Here, André Richard – who before the war had been a singer with the Paris Opera – recounts his experience in the Resistance.

I have never known any assignment that was not a dangerous one during the Occupation. Besides, in my opinion, this is what makes the true Resistance fighters so valuable, as they remained in direct contact with the enemy throughout the Occupation. These are what I call true Resistance fighters....

Now the resistance developed because we were a group of companions, all of us with a heavy heart, and I saw, and just as I did, many companions saw the Germans come into Paris with tears in our eyes. I mean that we had tears in our eyes when we saw the Germans come into Paris. Well, we remembered . . . the war of 1876 when the Germans, right, walked into Paris and, of course, we remembered this very day, thinking that our grandfathers had known the same suffering as we did, and this is when many of us had the idea, right, to say: but why don't we organize groups to meet and pull down everything the Germans might do, to make ourselves useful....

And quite often, quite often, these people . . . indeed, to my knowledge, those I have worked with, few of them returned alive. I can even say that when the Maintenon tunnel . . . blew up in Rouen with the trains . . . blew up, and also in Rouen with the ammunition loaded trains, well none of them returned, not anyone, not anyone . . . and I had to come home by myself and report to my leaders, right, report to Colonel Goisé and to Roger Bordé, right, Major Bordé, I had to come back by myself and tell him, right, what . . . what I had learned and how it had happened, well the information I had been given, and very often did I come back alone, while twenty of us had gone, and I came back alone from these assignments, which were really perilous.

1. What motivated Richard and his friends to join the Resistance?

2. Describe one assignment Richard helped to carry out.

3. Based on this excerpt, what qualities do you think a person needed to serve in the Resistance?

Source 3

Images of the Invasion of the Soviet Union

The Nazis first invaded the Soviet Union in June 1941. The turning point in the Soviet battle against the Nazis was the Battle of Stalingrad. From September 1942 to February 1943, soldiers and civilians in Stalingrad resisted the German invasion. There were more than 2 million casualties. But in the end, the frozen and starving invaders surrendered and the Soviets began driving the Nazis westward across Eastern Europe and back toward Germany.

Soviet guardsmen fire upon attacking German riflemen in Stalingrad.

These Soviet women served as guerrillas during the German invasion.

1. What does the photo on the left show you about the impact of the Soviet invasion on Stalingrad?

2. What role do you think the women on the right played during the Nazi invasion?

3. Why do you think these soldiers and civilians fought so fiercely against the German army?

Source 4

Frances Slanger, Letter from an American Nurse, published in Stars and Stripes, October 1944

Frances Slanger, a Jewish immigrant from Poland, joined the U.S. Army Nurse Corps in 1943. She asked to be sent to Europe and was one of four military nurses to land at Normandy on D-Day. In October 1944, she sent the following letter to the Army magazine *Stars and Stripes*. The same day, she was killed by a German sniper.

We had read several articles in different magazines and papers sent in by grateful GIs praising the work of the nurses around the combat zones. Praising us - for what?

We wade ankle-deep in mud - you have to lie in it. We are restricted to our immediate area, a cow pasture or a hay field, but then who is not restricted?

We have a stove and coal. We even have a laundry line in the tent.

The wind is howling, the tent waving precariously, the rain beating down, the guns firing, and me with a flashlight writing. It all adds up to a feeling of unreality. Sure we rough it, but in comparison to the way you men are taking it, we can't complain nor do we feel that bouquets are due us. But you - the men behind the guns, the men driving our tanks, flying our planes, sailing our ships, building bridges - it is to you we doff our helmets. To every GI wearing the American uniform, for you we have the greatest admiration and respect.

Yes, this time we are handing out the bouquets - but after taking care of some of your buddies, comforting them when they are brought in, bloody, dirty with the earth, mud and grime, and most of them so tired. Somebody's brothers, somebody's fathers, somebody's sons, seeing them gradually brought back to life, to consciousness, and their lips separate into a grin when they first welcome you....

These soldiers stay with us but a short time, from ten days to possibly two weeks. We have learned a great deal about our American boy and the stuff he is made of. The wounded do not cry. Their buddies come first. The patience and determination they show, the courage and fortitude they have is sometimes awesome to behold. It is we who are proud of you.

1. How do you think Slanger's background influenced her desire to serve as a nurse in Europe?

2. According to the letter, what are some of the hardships Army nurses faced? How does Slanger feel about them?

3. What was Slanger's main purpose in writing this letter and sending it to *Stars and Stripes*?

Lesson 1 A New Global Conflict

CLOSE READING

Wartime Alliance Breaks Apart

1. **Analyze Word Choices** What does *cold* in the term *Cold War* mean?

Soviet Aggression Grows

2. **Analyze Word Choices** Why did Churchill call the divide between East and West the "Iron Curtain"? Explain the symbolism of both *iron* and *curtain*.

Two Opposing Sides in Europe

3. **Identify Supporting Details** In the graphic organizer below, list the different ways in which Eastern Europeans reacted against Soviet domination and how the Soviets responded to their actions.

	East Germany (1953)	Hungary (1956)	Czechoslovakia (1968)
Reaction			
Soviet Response			

The Nuclear Arms Race

4. **Compare and Contrast** Use the information in the infographic to answer this question: Why was the SALT II Treaty stronger than the Nuclear Test Ban Treaty?

The Cold War Around the World

5. **Use Visual Information** In the graphic organizer below, identify the Cold War "hotspots" by region.

Central America	Middle East	East Asia	Africa

The Soviet Union During the Cold War

6. **Compare and Contrast** How did the leadership of Nikita Khrushchev differ from that of Joseph Stalin?

The United States in the Cold War

7. **Draw Inferences** What are the benefits of a market economy?

Lesson 2 The Western Democracies and Japan

CLOSE READING

Postwar Prosperity in the United States

1. **Cite Evidence** Give some examples of the new role played by the United States in the world after World War II.

2. **Draw Inferences** Why did Americans begin moving to the suburbs in the 1950s and 1960s?

The United States Responds to New Challenges

3. **Determine Meaning** What is the difference between discrimination and segregation?

4. **Cite Evidence** In what ways were minorities denied equality and opportunity in the United States in the 1950s and 1960s?

5. **Using Visual Information** Look at the chart of military spending in the United States. By how much did military spending increase from 1980 to 1990?

Rebuilding Western Europe

6. **Compare** the post-war experiences of West and East Germany.

Japan Is Transformed

7. **Cite Evidence** Give examples of policies Americans introduced during the occupation of Japan.

8. **Identify Cause and Effect** Why did Japan enjoy a trade surplus?

Lesson 3 Communism in East Asia

CLOSE READING

The Chinese Communist Victory

1. **Identify Supporting Details** Why did Chinese peasants support Mao Zedong?

2. **Summarize** What happened to the opponents of the Communist Party in China?

3. **Analyze Interaction** Why did Mao decide to stop the Cultural Revolution?

China and the Cold War

4. **Analyze Word Choices** What does it mean that the United States "played the China card"?

5. Compare and Contrast How was Jiang Jieshi's government in Taiwan similar to Mao Zedong's in Communist China?

The Two Koreas

6. Analyze Interactions Based on the map of the Korean Peninsula in the fall of 1950 and other events in Asia, and remembering what was happening in the rest of Asia, what risk did UN troops take when attacking North Korea?

7. Determine Central Ideas How would you describe Kim Il Sung as a leader? Give specific evidence from the text.

8. Summarize What are some differences between North Korea and South Korea?

Lesson 4 War in Southeast Asia

CLOSE READING

The Road to War in Southeast Asia

1. Identify Main Ideas Record the major events in Vietnam for each year below.

1946	1954	1959

2. Identify Supporting Details Why was Ngo Dinh Diem an unpopular ruler?

The United States Enters the War

3. Sequence What events led to American involvement in Vietnam?

4. Integrate Information from Diverse Sources Based on the map and the text, why might the United States have wanted to attack targets in Cambodia?

The Vietnam War Ends

5. Categorize In the graphic organizer below, list the reasons U.S. leaders might have given for and against continuing the war in Vietnam.

Reasons to Continue Fighting	Reasons to Pull Out

6. Assess an Argument Did the domino theory prove to be correct? Explain.

7. Identifying Supporting Details Give three reasons why many Vietnamese people might have wanted to leave Vietnam after the war.

Lesson 5 The Cold War Ends

CLOSE READING

The Soviet Union Declines

1. **Identify Supporting Details** How did the arms race put pressure on the Soviet economy?

2. **Cite Evidence** In the graphic organizer below, list the weaknesses of the Soviet political and economic systems.

Political Weaknesses	Economic Weaknesses

3. **Compare and Contrast** How was the Soviet war in Afghanistan similar to the Vietnam War?

The Soviet Union Collapses

4. **Draw Inferences** Why did Gorbachev's reforms cause economic turmoil in the Soviet Union?

Eastern Europe Transformed

5. **Determine Central Ideas** Why were Eastern European reforms allowed to happen in the late 1980s? What had happened before when Eastern Europeans attempted reform?

Communism Declines Around the World

6. **Cite Evidence** Were economic or political reforms more common as countries moved away from communism? Cite evidence to support your answer.

The Post–Cold War World

7. **Identify Cause and Effect** What was one effect of the recession of 2008 in Europe?

PRIMARY SOURCE EXPLORATION

The Cold War and Popular Culture

Introduction

For forty-four years, the Cold War was a period of competition, tension, and mutual hostilities between the Soviet Union and the United States and their respective allies. This was also a time when both sides used strategies to promote what they considered the advantages of their political systems. Popular culture became the way to communicate these ideas and to win hearts and minds.

Document-Based Writing Activity

Analyze the following four sources and then use information from the documents and your knowledge of world history to write an essay in which you

- Describe how the Cold War started. How did it affect the world?
- Discuss how the Cold War affected popular culture.

Keep in mind that your essay should include an introduction, several paragraphs, and a conclusion. In the body of the essay, use evidence from at least three documents. Support your response with relevant facts, examples, and details. In developing your essay, be sure to keep these general definitions in mind:

- *Describe* means "to illustrate something in words or tell about it."
- *Discuss* means "to make observations about something using facts, reasoning, and argument; to present in some detail."

Source 1

The Soviet Union Banned These Bands in 1985

During the 1970s, when intense international relations had somewhat relaxed during the Cold War, there was a rise of Western music and culture in the Soviet Union. As a result, young people in the Soviet Union enjoyed the music of the Beatles and the catchy sounds of hard rock. The Komsomol, the Soviet youth wing of the Communist Party, tried to control the growing popularity of Western music in the Soviet Union. Their goal was to create ideological guidelines for listening to Western music. Below is part of the banned list of Western artists prepared by the Komsomol.

NOT RECOMMENDED

THE BAND	THE REASON
Alice Cooper	Violence, vandalism
Scorpion	Violence
Genghis Khan	Anti-communism, nationalism
UFO	Violence
Talking Heads	Myth of Soviet military danger
B-52	Punk, violence
Pink Floyd	Interfering with the foreign policy of USSR (Afghanistan)

Source: SPIN

1. How do the reasons banning Western artists reflect Soviet views of the West during the Cold War?

2. Why do you think the Komsomol urged the opening of discos in the Soviet Union?

3. Eventually, some young people in the Soviet Union began to form their own bands. How do you think these bands were received? Explain.

Source 2

Evolution of Korean Anti-communist Films and its Conditions, Jo Jun-hyeong, 2011

In May 1960, Park Chung-hee took control of the South Korean government through a bloodless coup. While Chung-hee is criticized for his harsh authoritarian rule, he is respected for his rigorous policies that led to successful economic growth in South Korea. He also successfully protected South Korea against communist North Korea. The following source discusses his focus on anti-communism.

After the May 16 Coup, the Park Chung-hee regime, anti-communism was made a national policy and anti-communist propaganda efforts went into full drive. In the meantime, the nation set out to pursue modernization driven by economic growth. The coupling of anti-communism and economic growth spurred full on competition for regime legitimacy between the two Koreas, and any activity considered an impediment to South Korea's economic growth, and in turn, benefitting North Korea was suppressed in the name of communism. Park Chung-hee deemed [felt that] cinema [was] an especially effective medium for propaganda and thus aimed to spread anti-communism by revising the Motion Pictures Act, strengthening film censorship and other institutional measures. Against this political and social backdrop, anti-communist films came to comprise [make up] a genre [a group or category] of their own and production reached its zenith [highest point]. The need for movies about political revolutions or national reconstruction was brought to attention after the May 16 Coup, and anti-communist films were produced in large numbers after 1962. Until 1966, large-scale war movies comprised the most dominant sub-genre of anti-communist films. This indicates that anti-communist films were consumed by moviegoers as entertainment rather than for their propagandistic purpose as intended by the government.

1. Why did anti-communism become a national policy?

2. How did Chung-hee manipulate the film industry?

3. Why do you think audiences began to view the movies more as entertainment than for the propaganda which it was meant to convey?

Source 3

A Forgotten Cold War Hockey Tale by Stephen Hardy and Andrew C. Holman, 2018

Both western countries and nations in the Soviet bloc viewed sports competition as a continuation of cold war politics. Any sports event became a symbolic struggle between the capitalist and communist systems.

In November, 1959, America's reigning senior amateur ice hockey champions, the Brockton "Wetzells" of Massachusetts, accepted an invitation to play five games at Moscow's grand Luzhniki Sports Palace. It was the height of the Cold War and amid high expectations, the Americans' performance left much to be desired. In fact, it was a disaster. The episode has long been forgotten, but it reveals a good deal about how global politics has, ever since, come to "color" friendly international sport.

The Brockton squad was a talented group. . . "I don't think we will win all of our games," a sanguine [confident] coach Louis Duhamel predicted after the team's arrival, "but I'm no pessimist either, because I know the strength and will power of our players." But strength and will came nowhere near skill.

In five games, the Americans gave up 62 goals and scored seven. Among the most disappointed were Russian fans, 10,000 of whom showed up for the first game, but whose numbers dwindled thereafter. A New York Times headline states "Ineptitude [having no skill] of U.S. Hockey Team Astonishes Moscow Spectators." The Cold War was raging and a year earlier, the U.S. and Russia had fashioned a "Soviet-American Agreement on Scientific, Technical and Cultural Exchanges," which provided for "meets" between the countries in eight different sports, including hockey.

The Brockton trip was cast as a promising overture toward a cultural understanding. To American eyes, that was fine as long as "understanding" meant a demonstrated superiority. For this reason, the tour was followed keenly by major media in the U.S. By the end of the tour, the press had vilified [criticized] the players as. . . poor ambassadors.

But the deepest embarrassment came less from the team's conduct than from its appalling loss to the Soviets at a time when sport had become a proxy for a political system's worth, "If we hope to impress the world," one letter to the editor wrote in the noted Sports Illustrated, "then we should send nothing but the best, for its eyes are on America and everything we do."

1. Why was the choice of a hockey team especially important in 1959?

2. Why do you think so many Russian fans showed up for the games?

3. The United States and the Soviet signed a Soviet-American Agreement on Scientific, Technical and Cultural Exchanges. How might both sides have gained from this agreement?

Source 4

McDonald's Comes to Moscow

As the world's most popular fast food restaurant, the first McDonald's arrived in Moscow in 1990. The venture was a success. After the end of the Cold War, American culture began to penetrate Soviet society. Shopping malls, nightclubs, and more fast-food restaurants became common. Shown here are Russians eating at McDonald's in 1997.

1. Based on the image, what changes seemed to have occurred after the arrival of McDonald's?

2. How would the introduction of the restaurant become a part of Gorbachev's perestroika and glasnost policies?

3. Do you think this affected the political situation between the United States and Russia? Explain.

Lesson 1 New Nations in South Asia and Southeast Asia

CLOSE READING

Independence and Partition in South Asia

1. **Identify Cause and Effect** Describe the events that led to the formation of an independent India and Pakistan.

Challenges to Modern India

2. **Summarize** Based on the text, what are some of the challenges that India has faced as the world's largest parliamentary democracy?

Pakistan and Bangladesh Separate

3. **Summarize** What economic and geographic factors led to the creation of an independent Bangladesh? Use evidence from the text to support your answer.

4. **Identify Supporting Details** The text states, "After independence, Pakistan struggled to build a stable government." Which details from the text support this statement?

South Asia in the Cold War

5. Identify Cause and Effect As you read "South Asia in the Cold War," use this graphic organizer to record one cause and one effect of the nonaligned movement.

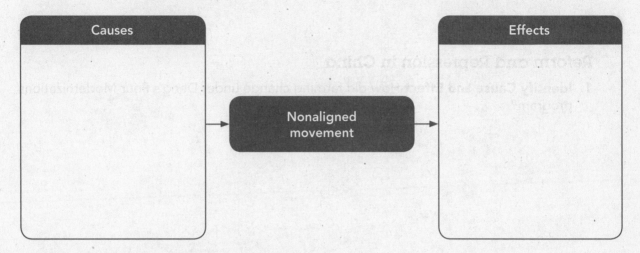

Independent Nations in Southeast Asia

6. Compare and Contrast Compare economic conditions in Malaysia to those of Myanmar. How is this difference in their economies linked to the wider differences between the two countries?

Populous Indonesia Faces Challenges

7. Synthesize How has diversity posed challenges to Indonesia?

Struggle for Democracy in the Philippines

8. Draw Inferences Why has economic growth in the Philippines been limited? Consider the factors that have been discussed in the text.

Lesson 2 Rapid Development in China and India

CLOSE READING

Reform and Repression in China

1. **Identify Cause and Effect** How did farming change under Deng's Four Modernizations program?

2. **Identify Central Issues** What were students and others protesting in Tiananmen Square?

Growth and Challenges

3. **Identify Cause and Effect** What are some of the effects that China is dealing with as a result of rapid urbanization?

4. **Synthesize Information** Why did some people think the one-child policy was a human rights abuse? In what ways did the policy help China?

India Builds a Modern Economy

5. Identify Central Issues How did the Green Revolution affect rural India?

6. Identify Details As you read, use the web to record details about the challenges India faces.

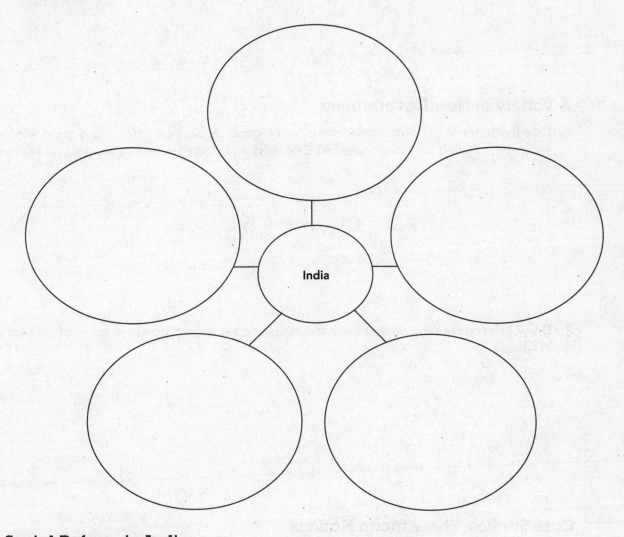

India

Social Reform in India

7. Cite Evidence Has discrimination against women in India lessened? What work is left to be done? Use textual evidence to support your answer.

Lesson 3 African Nations Win Independence

CLOSE READING

The New Nations of Africa

1. **Summarize** Why did African nations gain independence after World War II?

A Variety of New Governments

2. **Cite Evidence** What circumstances led to the conflicts between ethnic groups in African nations struggling for independence? Cite evidence from the text to support your answer.

3. **Draw Inferences** Why do you think the military often seized power in areas of civil unrest in Africa?

Case Studies: Five African Nations

4. **Identify Effects** How have Nigeria's rich oil resources caused problems?

5. **Compare and Contrast** Compare and contrast the history of national independence in two of the nations in this section (Ghana, Kenya, Algeria, Democratic Republic of Congo, and Nigeria). Consider political, economic, and geographic causes, as well as conflicts among religious and ethnic groups. Also, look at where the path to independence has led for two of these nations. Fill in the chart below to organize your information.

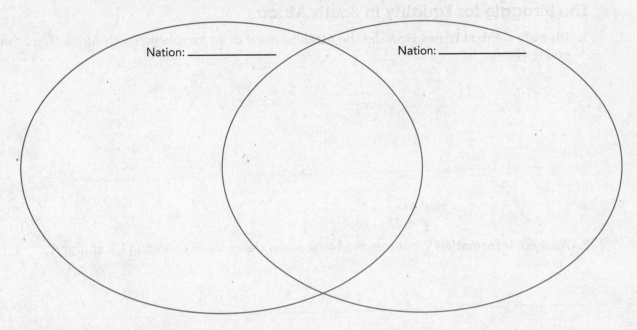

Nation: _____   Nation: _____

The Wars of Southern Africa

6. **Draw Inferences** How did the Cold War affect independence in Angola and Mozambique?

Ethnic Conflict and Genocide

7. **Identify Supporting Details** The text states that "Regional and cultural differences also fed rivalries" that led to violence. Which details from the text support this statement?

Lesson 4 Challenges for African Nations

CLOSE READING

The Struggle for Equality in South Africa

1. **Identify Central Issues** How did the establishment of white rule in South Africa affect the country?

2. **Analyze Information** What role did Nelson Mandela play in changing his country?

3. **Compare and Contrast** What was life like for Black South Africans during and after apartheid?

African Nations Face Economic Choices

4. **Identify Effects** Why did most African countries move towards a market-driven economy in the 1980s?

5. Summarize Why have the economies of some African nations improved in recent years?

Ongoing Challenges

6. Identify Main Ideas As you read this section, fill in the chart below with information about ongoing challenges for African nations.

Urbanization	Environmental Issues	Disease	Conflict

Lesson 5 The Modern Middle East Takes Shape

CLOSE READING

The Challenges of Diversity

1. **Analyze** How did the mandates after World War I contribute to tensions in the Middle East?

2. **Vocabulary: Determine Meaning** Read "Kurdish Nationalism." What do you think the word *autonomy* means? What does it mean when the text states that "Today, Kurds in Iraq have much autonomy, but many Kurds still want their own state"?

The Founding of Israel

3. **Hypothesize** Do you think the 1948 war ended the conflict between Israel and Palestinian Arabs? Why or why not?

4. **Understand Main Ideas** Why was the "right of return" important to the Jewish people?

New Nations in the Middle East

5. Summarize Describe the Arab Spring and its effects.

6. Identify Cause and Effect What have been the effects of political changes in Iran since 1951?

The Importance of Oil in the Middle East

7. Draw Inferences Read the information about the Organization of Petroleum Exporting Countries (OPEC). Based on what you've read, what is the effect of OPEC's production quotas on the global economy?

Islam and the Modern World

8. Analyze Based on the text, what is the relationship between Islam and the various governments in the Middle East? Cite evidence from the text to support your answer.

9. Draw Inferences Read the quote from paragraph three of "Islam and the Lives of Women." What does this quote tell you about women in the Middle East and the Arab Spring?

"I grew up in a world where we believed we could not do anything. Generations believed we could do nothing, and now, in a matter of weeks, we know that we can."

Lesson 6 Conflicts in the Middle East

CLOSE READING

Israel and Palestine

1. **Hypothesize** What is the connection between Arab defeats in wars against Israel and the use of guerrilla war and intifadas by some Palestinians?

2. **Summarize** Consider the causes and effects of the long-standing conflict between Israel and the Palestinians. Complete the chart with this information.

Causes	Effects

The Difficult Road to Peace

3. **Summarize** What, according to the text, are the four main obstacles to peace between Israel and Palestinians?

4. **Hypothesize** Why do you think Iran and radical Islamist groups have rejected the two-state plan?

Conflict in Lebanon and Syria

5. Identify Supporting Details What conditions led to the Lebanese Civil War? Cite supporting details from the text.

6. Draw Inferences Based on the text, how has the extremist group Hezbollah affected the stability of the Middle East?

Warfare in Iraq

7. Analyze Why did the United States become involved in the Iran-Iraq war?

8. Draw Inferences Why has the violence in Iraq continued, even after the withdrawal of American troops in 2011?

Lesson 7 Latin American Nations Move Towards Democracy

CLOSE READING

Challenges to Development

1. **Identify Cause and Effect** What impact did relying on a single cash crop have on Latin American economies?

2. **Infer** How does inequality hurt Latin American economies?

Dictators and Civil War

3. **Cite Evidence** Which groups in Latin America pressed for reforms starting in the 1950s? Use details from the text to support your answer.

4. **Identify Cause and Effect** What did military leaders in many Latin American nations do once they had gained power?

5. Identify Cause and Effect What major shift resulted from elections in Brazil, Venezuela, and Bolivia in the 1990s?

Latin America and the United States

6. Determine Point of View How do the United States and Latin American countries view their relationship with one another?

7. Analyze Information The United States supported the Bay of Pigs invasion in Cuba. Using this example, explain the main reason the United States intervened in Latin American countries during the Cold War.

The Long Road to Democracy in Argentina

8. Make Inferences What can you infer from the fact that military governments were in and out of power in Argentina for several decades?

PRIMARY SOURCE EXPLORATION

Economic Development in Independent Africa

Introduction

Economic development is a vitally important issue in new and developing countries. Many developing countries follow a mixed model of economic development, using features of both socialism and capitalism. In post-World War II Africa, as in other parts of the developing world, newly independent nations faced the challenges of poverty, unemployment, urbanization, the need for agricultural development, and the appropriate use of natural resources. As they developed, African governments and people had to decide how best to pursue economic growth and modernization.

Document-Based Writing Activity

Analyze the following four sources and then use information from the documents and your knowledge of world history to write an essay in which you

- Discuss some of the issues involved in economic development in developing regions.

Keep in mind that your essay should include an introduction, several paragraphs, and a conclusion. In the body of the essay, use evidence from at least three documents. Support your response with relevant facts, examples, and details. In developing your essay, be sure to keep this general definition in mind:

- *Discuss* means "to make observations about something using facts, reasoning, and argument; to present in some detail."

Source 1

The Arusha Declaration, Julius Nyerere, translated from Swahili, 1967

Julius Nyerere was the first president of independent Tanzania. In 1967, he laid out his vision for his country's future in the Arusha Declaration, excerpted below. Nyerere believed in African socialism, which focused on cooperation and self-reliance. In the Arusha Declaration, he advocated for the development of agriculture and called on all citizens to work together to achieve economic development.

It is obvious that in the past we have chosen the wrong weapon for our struggle, because we chose money as our weapon. We are trying to overcome our economic weakness by using the weapons of the economically strong—weapons which in fact we do not possess. . . .

The mistake we are making is to think that development begins with industries. It is a mistake because we do not have the means to establish many modern industries in our country. We do not have either the necessary finances or the technical know-how. It is not enough to say that we shall borrow the finances and the technicians from other countries to come and start the industries. . . .

The development of a country is brought about by people, not by money. Money, and the wealth it represents, is the result and not the basis of development.

A great part of Tanzania's land is fertile and gets sufficient rains. Our country can produce various crops for home consumption and for export. We can produce food crops (which can be exported if we produce in large quantities). . . . And because the main aim of our development is to get more food, and more money for our other needs, our purpose must be to increase production of these agricultural crops. This is in fact the only road through which we can develop our country—in other words, only by increasing our production of these things can we get more food and more money for every Tanzanian. . . .

What we are saying, however, is that from now on we shall know what is the foundation and what is the fruit of development. Between money and people it is obvious that the people and their hard work are the foundation of development, and money is one of the fruits of that hard work.

From now on we shall stand upright and walk forward on our feet rather than look at this problem upside down. Industries will come and money will come, but their foundation is the people and their hard work, especially in agriculture. This is the meaning of self-reliance.

---

1. According to Nyerere, what is the main aim of Tanzania's development?

2. What is the foundation of development, according to this source?

3. In your own words, summarize the last paragraph of the source.

Source 2

Ogoni-Shell Correspondence, 1970

Beginning in the 1950s, multinational corporations like the Shell-BP Oil Company expanded their oil extraction operations in the oil-rich Niger Delta. Oil production helped make the Nigerian economy one of the largest in Africa—but it also brought problems. In 1970, Nigeria's Ogoni people wrote to the state governor demanding relief from Shell-BP's actions. Read an excerpt from their letter and the Shell-BP response below.

[From Ogoni Chief] While it is a fact of history that the petroleum oil industry has given the national economy of Nigeria a great leap forward, it is equally and sadly true that neither the nation nor the Shell-BP Company has ever given serious and deserved consideration to the effects which this industry has had, and will continue to have, on the economy and life of the people of this Division, which has become the main home of the oil industry in Nigeria. . . .

About two decades ago, agriculture was the mainstay of the economy of Ogoni Division. But today, the entire economy of our people has been completely disrupted through the connivance of a nation which seems to have allowed the Shell-BP, a purely commercial organization, to enter upon and seize the people's land at will. . . . Deprived thus of his only source of income, the dispossessed farmer is ruined, and his children can no longer obtain an education nor his family a decent life. . . .

A few years ago, our streams were blessed with pure and sparkling water. But in the Gokana area of the Division, most inland waters, rivers and water courses have today been polluted by crude oil, mud, and other fluids which have contaminated our water supply. . . .

[Response from Shell-BP] As with any special pleading, the petition exaggerates or misrepresents in one direction (e.g. the amount of land occupied for oil operations in Ogoni Division) and minimizes in the other (e.g. the amount of compensation paid by Shell-BP in Ogoni Division over the past years). There can be no doubt, however, that the incidental benefits accruing to Ogoni Division from Shell-BP's presence there greatly outweighs any disadvantages. . . .

1. In your own words, summarize the first paragraph of the Ogoni chief's letter.

2. According to the Ogoni chief, how has the oil industry affected his people?

3. Do you think both the Ogonis' and Shell-BP's claims could be valid? Explain your reasoning.

Source 3

Account of Auntie Afriyie, Published in African Market Women, Gracia Clark, 2010

Female small business owners, or market women, play a critical role in West African economies. American anthropologist Gracia Clark recorded the life stories of seven entrepreneurs in Ghana. The excerpt below tells the story of Auntie Afriyie, who explains the culture of the market and how she became successful.

GC: What did you do to learn how to sell palm nuts?

It is wisdom.

GC: Is there any relative that came to sell palm nuts, and you followed her?

That sister of my mother's, she came first to sell and I came to join her. It was my sister who came to join her, and when my sister came to join her, she herself sold avocados and oranges. So I too, when I arrived, sold avocados and oranges. But when I examined it carefully, it was not good. But I sold some of the palm nuts, and they did better than the avocados. What came into my mind was that I should go and sell palm nuts. . . .

Also, when I went to the farm with my mother and went where they had cut them, and there were some left behind, my mother would go on and I would sit down to pick them up. Maybe I would get about a basketful. . . . So when I picked them up like that, and took them to show to my mother, she would pick out some and we made soup with them. I would go out with the rest and retail them for a penny. That made me know that there was profit in palm nuts. . . .

GC: Your machine, that you brought to press the oil, are you the only one that uses it, or can someone come to hire it to press hers?

If someone comes, I will not give it to her. For people can come to tell me that they want to hire it and use it, and I say you won't get a chance. When the palm nuts are plentiful every day, I will boil them. So you want to take my machine to put yours in it? I will not do that, because when it breaks down, it is manpower, I have to send it off to maintenance. So I use it myself for my own goods, little by little. . . .

When the rain falls on palm nuts, they get very hot inside the sack or the basket. If today it gets rained on, the next day you put your hand inside and ah, it burns you and it clumps together. It is not spoiled. The water has cooked it, *wahu?* . . . But the person who is buying it will tell you that it is rotten. So then, I gather my goods and put them in a pot, and when I put it on the fire, it cooks very fast. Then I pound it and pick the kernels out and I press it. *Wahu?* So I am always wiser than them. . . . If you are not wise, you cannot live in Ghana. . . .

1. What did Auntie Afriyie first sell?

2. How did Auntie Afriyie's work change over time?

3. What does she mean by saying "If you are not wise, you cannot live in Ghana"?

Source 4

Nigeria's Poverty Rate and Oil Income

Nigeria has one of the largest economies in Africa, primarily due to its oil industry. Oil extraction has created many jobs and made some people very wealthy, but the country's reliance on oil has also created problems, with the economy rising and falling as global oil prices fluctuate. In the early 1970s, when the Nigerian economy expanded due to rising oil prices, workers moved to urban centers for new job opportunities. As a result, agriculture declined and by 1975, Nigeria had to import much of the food the country needed.

Poverty Rate

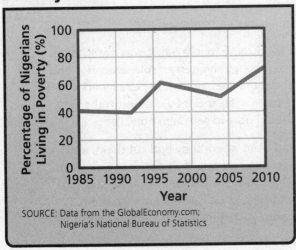

SOURCE: Data from the GlobalEconomy.com;
Nigeria's National Bureau of Statistics

Income from Oil Sales

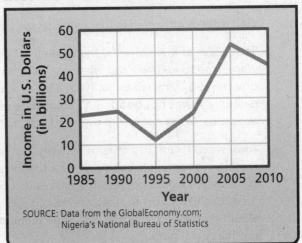

SOURCE: Data from the GlobalEconomy.com;
Nigeria's National Bureau of Statistics

1. What does the graph on the left show?

2. What does the graph on the right show?

3. Taken together, what do these graphs suggest about the role of the oil industry in Nigeria's economy?

Lesson 1 The Developing World

CLOSE READING

Working Toward Development

1. **Identify Supporting Details** Read the two paragraphs under "Uneven Development." Notice that the text states that "Developing countries include a wide range of different economies." What details from the text support this statement?

2. **Summarize** What factors have affected the success of developing countries in their efforts to develop?

Challenges to Development

3. **Analyze** Read the section "Rising Populations." What is the relationship between population and progress in developing countries?

4. Draw Conclusions What factors have posed obstacles to some countries' development?

Development Brings Social Change

5. Generate Explanations Why do the rural poor in many developing countries move to cities? How might they be persuaded to remain in their rural homes?

6. Identify Cause and Effect What have been some of the effects of economic development in the developing world? Use the chart to organize your answer.

Cause	Effect
• Opportunities for women have increased in developing nations.	
• Families move to cities and take low-paying jobs.	
• Religious revivals have swept many developing nations.	
• People have flooded into cities to escape rural poverty.	

Lesson 2 The More Developed World

CLOSE READING

A New Europe

1. **Draw Inferences** What challenges did Germany face at the end of the Cold War?

2. **Identify Cause and Effect** As you read "Wars in the Balkans," examine the text for clues that signal cause and effect. Then use a chart like this one to record major causes and effects of conflicts in that region.

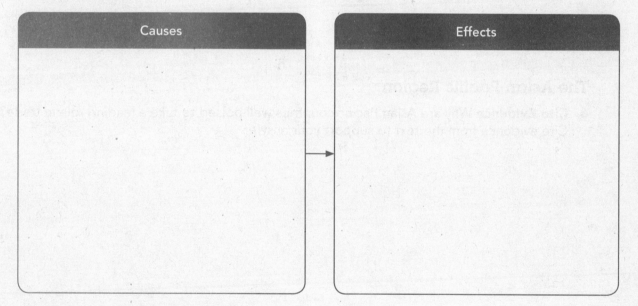

Causes	Effects

Russia and Its Neighbors

3. **Summarize** What were the effects of Vladimir Putin's rule in Russia? Why have some people criticized his leadership?

The United States Faces New Challenges

4. Identify Cause and Effect How did President Obama respond to the 2008 financial crisis, and what was the effect of his response?

5. Analyze How did polarization affect the United States?

The Asian Pacific Region

6. Cite Evidence Why are Asian Pacific countries well poised to take a leading role in trade? Cite evidence from the text to support your answer.

7. Predict Consequences Which country or countries do you think will dominate the global economy in the coming years? Why do you think so?

Lesson 3 Globalization and Trade

CLOSE READING

Global Interdependence

1. **Summarize** What is globalization? What are three ways countries of the world depend on one another?

2. **Identify Cause and Effect** As you read "Global Economic Crises," use this graphic organizer to record the causes and effects of the global economic downturn in 2008–2009.

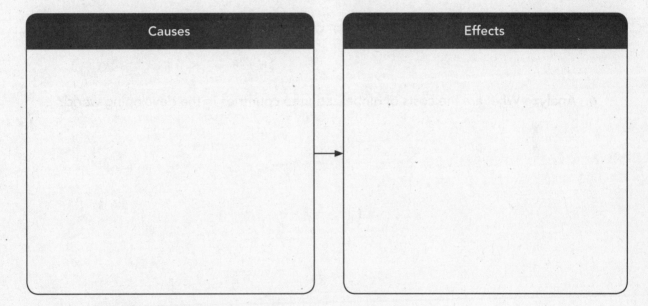

Causes	Effects

Global Organizations and Trade Agreements

3. **Cite Evidence** Explain the role and significance of the United Nations. Cite evidence from the text to support your answer.

4. **Explain** How does the World Trade Organization work to promote international trade?

Challenges to Globalization

5. **Compare and Contrast** How do the benefits of globalization differ in developing and developed countries?

6. **Analyze** What are the costs of globalization to countries in the developing world?

7. **Hypothesize** How do you think people in the anti-globalization movement can effect change in multinational corporations?

Lesson 4 Social and Environmental Issues

CLOSE READING

Global Challenges

1. **Integrate Information From Diverse Sources** Read "Worldwide Poverty." Then look at the world map showing per capita GDP. What do the text and map convey about the status of nations around the world?

2. **Identify Cause and Effect** As you read "People Search for a Better Life," use this graphic organizer to record the causes and effects of migration. What causes people to move? What are the effects?

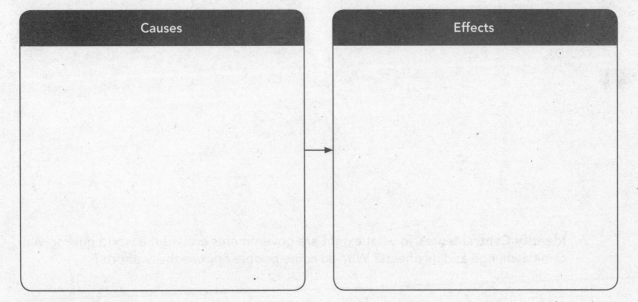

Causes	Effects

Human Rights

3. **Infer** Why might human rights abuses continue to occur despite the UN Universal Declaration of Human Rights and the Helsinki Accords?

4. Cite Evidence What information supports the idea that women around the world still suffer from unequal treatment? Use evidence from the text to support your answer.

Development and the Environment

5. Summarize In what ways can rapid development threaten the environment?

6. Identify Central Issues To what extent are governments around the world dealing with climate change and its effects? Why do some people oppose these efforts?

Lesson 5 International Security

CLOSE READING

The Threat of Deadly Weapons

1. **Analyze Information** How does the Nuclear Nonproliferation Treaty attempt to deal with weapons of mass destruction around the world?

2. **Draw Conclusions** Why are people concerned about terrorists acquiring weapons of mass destruction?

Terrorism and the U.S. Response

3. **Summarize** What actions did the United States take as a direct response to the attacks of September 11, 2001? Cite textual evidence to support your answer.

4. **Cite Evidence** Which source of terrorism do you consider the greatest threat to the United States? Cite evidence from the text to support your answer.

Aggressive Governments

5. Draw Conclusions Why has Russian aggression been a cause for concern to the United States and other nations?

6. Compare and Contrast Compare and contrast the risks to global stability posed by Russia, China, Iran, and North Korea.

New Risks Emerge

7. Identify Cause and Effect How might global climate change be connected to global migration?

Lesson 6 Advances in Science and Technology

CLOSE READING

Space Exploration

1. Cite Evidence What are scientists currently doing to learn more about space? Cite textual evidence to support your answer.

2. Summarize What are three categories of artificial satellites, and what kinds of information do we get from each?

The Digital Revolution

3. Integrate Information From Diverse Sources Read "The Birth of Computers." Then look at the picture of early computers. What do the text and photo convey about how computers have improved since their creation?

4. Identify Cause and Effect How has the Internet shaped our world?

Breakthroughs in Medicine and Biotechnology

5. Infer Computers have aided doctors in diagnosing and treating diseases. What does this suggest about the role of computers in medicine in the future?

6. Identify Central Ideas What two approaches did doctors and medical scientists use to fight COVID-19?

Standards of Living Rise

7. Summarize What have been the biggest benefits of science and technology in our world?

PRIMARY SOURCE EXPLORATION

Protecting the Rights of Children

Introduction

Today, about 25 percent of the world's population is under the age of 15—roughly 1.9 billion children. And nearly half of them live in poverty, especially in developing nations. Warfare, disease, abuse, lack of education—these are among the global challenges that hit children the hardest. At the same time, organizations and individuals are working hard to protect the rights of the world's children.

Document-Based Writing Activity

Analyze the following three sources and then use information from the documents and your knowledge of world history to write an essay in which you

- Describe some of the basic rights that children should have.
- Evaluate the efforts individuals and organizations have made to protect children's rights.

Keep in mind that your essay should include an introduction, several paragraphs, and a conclusion. In the body of the essay, use evidence from at least three documents. Support your response with relevant facts, examples, and details. In developing your essay, be sure to keep these general definitions in mind:

- *Describe* means "to illustrate something in words or tell about it."
- *Evaluate* means "to examine and judge the significance, worth, or condition of; to determine the value of."

Source 1

Convention on the Rights of the Child

The United Nations adopted the Convention on the Rights of the Child in 1989. It has been ratified by every member nation except the United States. The treaty defines a child as anyone under the age of 18, except in countries where the legal age is younger. These are some of the many provisions of the treaty.

- States Parties [or nations that ratify the convention] shall take measures to combat the illicit transfer and non-return of children abroad....

- States Parties shall respect the right of the child to freedom of thought, conscience and religion....

- No child shall be subjected to arbitrary or unlawful interference with his or her privacy, family, home or correspondence, nor to unlawful attacks on his or her honour and reputation....

- States Parties recognize that a mentally or physically disabled child should enjoy a full and decent life, in conditions which ensure dignity, promote self-reliance and facilitate the child's active participation in the community....

- States Parties recognize the right of the child to the enjoyment of the highest attainable standard of health and to facilities for the treatment of illness and rehabilitation of health. States Parties shall strive to ensure that no child is deprived of his or her right of access to such health care services....

- States Parties recognize the right of every child to a standard of living adequate for the child's physical, mental, spiritual, moral and social development....

- States Parties recognize the right of the child to education, and with a view to achieving this right progressively and on the basis of equal opportunity, they shall, in particular: Make primary education compulsory and available free to all....

- States Parties recognize the right of the child to rest and leisure, to engage in play and recreational activities appropriate to the age of the child and to participate freely in cultural life and the arts....

- States Parties recognize the right of the child to be protected from economic exploitation and from performing any work that is likely to be hazardous or to interfere with the child's education, or to be harmful to the child's health or physical, mental, spiritual, moral or social development....

1. Which provision above might mean that every child is entitled to warm clothing and safe housing?

2. A child works twelve hours a day in a factory, then goes home, does household chores, and goes to bed. Which provisions would this violate?

3. Which of the provisions do you think should apply to adults as well as to children?

Source 2

Graph on Child Labor and Photograph of Child Labor Protest

Since the Industrial Revolution, most Western nations have passed laws regulating child labor. However, child labor is still a pressing issue in many parts of the world, especially the developing nations of Asia, Africa, and Latin America. These images highlight modern child labor trends and efforts to end the practice.

Worldwide Child Labor, 2000-2016

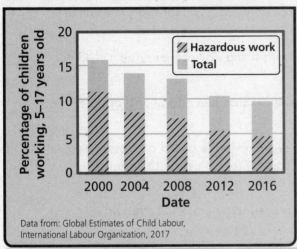

Data from: Global Estimates of Child Labour, International Labour Organization, 2017

This graph shows the percentage of the world's children working, over a span of 16 years. The majority of these children worked in agriculture.

This protest against child labor took place in Amritsar, India. Similar protests have taken place in many other nations.

1. In 2000, there were approximately 1.5 billion children in the world. According to the graph, how many of these children worked? How many worked in hazardous jobs?

2. Which has declined more, the percentage of children in hazardous jobs or the overall percentage of children working?

3. What impact do you think protests like the one shown here might have had on the statistics shown on the graph?

Source 3

Malala Yousafzai: 16th-birthday speech at the United Nations, 2013

At 15, Malala Yousafzai was shot in the head by members of the Taliban, a radical Islamist group. They opposed her efforts to insure education for girls in Pakistan. She recovered and continued to speak out. The following year, Yousafzai became the youngest recipient of the Nobel Peace Prize. On her 16th birthday, she addressed the United Nations.

We call upon all governments to ensure free compulsory education for every child all over the world.

We call upon all governments to fight against terrorism and violence, to protect children from brutality and harm.

We call upon the developed nations to support the expansion of educational opportunities for girls in the developing world.

We call upon all communities to be tolerant—to reject prejudice based on caste, creed, sect, religion or gender. To ensure freedom and equality for women so that they can flourish. We cannot all succeed when half of us are held back.

We call upon our sisters around the world to be brave—to embrace the strength within themselves and realize their full potential.

Dear brothers and sisters, we want schools and education for every child's bright future. We will continue our journey to our destination of peace and education for everyone. No one can stop us. We will speak for our rights and we will bring change through our voice. We must believe in the power and the strength of our words. Our words can change the world.

Because we are all together, united for the cause of education. And if we want to achieve our goal, then let us empower ourselves with the weapon of knowledge and let us shield ourselves with unity and togetherness.

Dear brothers and sisters, we must not forget that millions of people are suffering from poverty, injustice and ignorance. We must not forget that millions of children are out of schools. We must not forget that our sisters and brothers are waiting for a bright peaceful future.

So let us wage a global struggle against illiteracy, poverty and terrorism and let us pick up our books and pens. They are our most powerful weapons.

One child, one teacher, one pen and one book can change the world.

Education is the only solution. Education first.

1. What was Yousafzai's goal in making this speech to this particular audience?

2. What does she think can be accomplished through education?

3. Why do you think Yousafzai was viewed as a hero by much of the world?

Photography

Topic 1
9TL: Adam Fichna/Shutterstock; **9TR:** Acceptphoto/Shutterstock; **9BL:** WildMedia/Shutterstock; **9BR:** Vagabond54/Shutterstock

Topic 2
21: Photo Researchers/Science History Images/Alamy Stock Photo

Topic 3
35: © Chungking/Fotolia

Topic 4
46: Icom Images/Alamy Stock Photo

Topic 5
59: Peter Horree/Alamy Stock Photo

Topic 6
73L: Hoberman Collection/Universal Images Group/Getty Images; **73R:** Adam Eastland/Alamy Stock Photo

Topic 7
95: Album/Alamy Stock Photo; **96:** Historic Images/Alamy Stock Photo

Topic 8
117: Reproduced from Horse in West African History (African Ethnographic Studies 20th Century), 1st Edition by Robin, Law, published by Routledge. © Reproduced by arrangement with Taylor & Francis Books UK

Topic 9
132: Purchase, W. M. Keck Foundation Gift and other gifts, in memory of Douglas Dillon, 2005/The Metropolitan Museum of Art

Topic 10
147: Heritage Image Partnership Ltd/Fine Art Images/Alamy Stock Photo

Topic 11
163: Photo Researchers/Science History Images/Alamy Stock Photo

Topic 13
200: Jean S. and Frederic A. Sharf Collection/Museum of Fine Arts, Boston

Topic 14
221: Pictorial Press Ltd/Alamy Stock Photo

Topic 15
242L: The Print Collector/Heritage Image/Age Fotostock; **242R:** Pictures From History/CPA Media Pte Ltd/Alamy Stock Photo

Topic 16
256L: Photo Researchers/Science History Images/Alamy Stock Photo; **256R:** Niday Picture Library/Alamy Stock Photo

Topic 18
291L: Sovfoto/Universal Images Group/Shutterstock; **291R:** Ron Harvey/Everett Collection Historical/Alamy Stock Photo

Topic 19
307: Andres Hernandez/Liaison/Hulton Archive/Getty Image

Topic 21
341: Narinder Nanu/AFP/Getty Images

Text Acknowledgements

Topic 1
"How Accurate Is Alpha's Theory of Dog Domestication?" by Brian Handwerk, Smithsonian magazine, August 15, 2018. Copyright 2018 Smithsonian Institution. Reprinted with permission from Smithsonian Enterprises. All rights reserved. Reproduction in any medium is strictly prohibited without permission from Smithsonian Institution.

Topic 2
Excerpt From: Charles F. Horne, The Sacred Books and Early Literature of the East (New York: Parke, Austin, & Lipscomb, 1917), Vol. II: Egypt, pp. 62–78.; Excerpt From Papyrus of Ani: Egyptian Book of the Dead translated by E. A. Wallis Budge published by G.P. Putnam's Sons, 1913.; Excerpt From The Tomb of Tutankhamen by Howard Carter and A.C. Mace. Published in 1923 by Cassell and Company, LTD.

Topic 3
Excerpt From Sources of Chinese Tradition, compiled by Wm. Theodore de Bary and Irene Bloom, 2nd ed., vol. 1 (New York: Columbia University Press, 1999), 208–210. © 1999 Columbia University Press. Reproduced with the permission of the publisher. All rights reserved.; Quote from Speech at the Eleventh Session of the Supreme State Conference. Mao Tsetung. People's Daily on June 19, 1957; Eyewitness of the Cultural

Revolution. The China Quarterly, No. 28 (Oct.–Dec., 1966), pp. 1–7.Published by Cambridge University Press on behalf of the School of Oriental and African Studies.

Topic 4

Excerpt From Annals of Native America: How the Nahuas of Colonial Mexico Kept Their History Alive by Camilla Townsend. © Oxford University Press 2017. Reprinted with permission.; Excerpt From Tlaxcalan Leaders Tell Cortes about the Mexicas and their History by Bernal Diaz del Castillo, Vol.2. Chapter 78. Historia verdadera de la conquista de la Nueva España. 4 vols. México: Oficina tipográfica de la Secretaría de fomento, 1904, 1905.; Excerpt From Excavations at Aztec Peasant Sites by Dr. Michael E. Smith and Cynthia Heath-Smith. Copyright © Dr. Michael E. Smith. Reprinted with permission.

Topic 5

NHK (Japan Broadcasting Corporation); 05: Excerpt from Antigone by Sophocles, translated by J.E. Thomas.; Excerpt from: Medea by Euripides, Translated by J.E. Thomas.

Topic 6

Excerpt From Augustus: First Emperor of Rome by Adrian Goldsworthy. Published by Yale University Press, 2014. Yale University Press, Copyright © 2014. Reprinted with permission.; Excerpt From Augustus: First Emperor of Rome by Adrian Goldsworthy. Published by Yale University Press, 2014. Yale University Press, Copyright © 2014. Reprinted with permission.; Excerpt From The Annals by Tacitus. Translated by Alfred John Church and William Jackson Brodbribb.; Excerpt From The Deeds of the Divine Augustus by Augustus Caesar. Translated by Thomas Bushnell, BSG. Copyright 1998 by Thomas Bushnell, BSG.

Topic 7

Excerpt From Vita S. Thomae, Cantuariensis Archepiscopi et Martyris, ed. in James Robertson, Materials for the Life of Thomas Becket, (London: Rolls Series, 1875–1885) (7 vols.) Vol. II. Translated by Dawn Marie Hayes, Ph.D. Reprinted with permission.; Excerpt from: The Church Historians of England, Vol IV Part II, page 480–481. Seeleys, 1857.; Excerpt from The Church Historians of England: Reformation Period, Volume 5, Part 1, p. 239. Seeleys, 1857.

Topic 8

Excerpt from: History of the Berbers and the Muslim Dynasties of North Africa, part of the Book of Lessons, Ibn Khaldun, c. 1400. Translated into French by Pearson Staff, 2020.; Ihediwa Nkemjika Chimee; The Empire of Mali by Sirio Canós-Donnay/Oxford University Press

Topic 9

Yang Wanli's poem in Song Dynasty Poems by John Knoepfle and Wang Shouyi.; Excerpt from The Inner Quarters: Marriage and the Lives of Chinese Woman in the Sung Period, edited by Patricia Buckley Ebrey. Published by The University of California Press.; Fan Chengda's poetry about rural life in "Boulder Lake Poems: Fan Chengda's (1126–1193) Rural Year in Suzhou Revisited," Chinese Literature: Essays, Articles, Reviews (CLEAR), Vol. 10, No. 1/2 (July, 1988). University of Wisconsin. Reprinted with permission

Topic 10

Excerpt from: "Il libro dell'arte (The Craftsmans Handbook)" by Cennino d'Andrea Cennini. Copyright © Dover Publications. Reprinted with permission.; Excerpt describing Lorenzo de Medici's School of Sculpture from: Lives of the Artists by Giorgio Vasari. Translated by Mrs. Foster. Christians Inscriptions by H.P.Nunn. The Mcmillan Company, 1920.; Michaelangelo: To Giovanni Da Pistoia When the Author Was Painting the Vault of the Sistine Chapel. From: Zeppo's First Wife : New and Selected Poems. Published by The University of Chicago Press. Reprinted with permission.

Topic 11

Excerpt from: The Trial of Captain Kidd (1701). Published by Willian Hodge and Co, Glasgow and Edinburgh 1930.; Excerpt from "A General History of the Pyrates". Published by T. Warner (1724); Quote from Report of the Secretary-General of the United Nations, 2010.; Quote from: "My 977 days held hostage by Somali pirates," Michael Scott Moore. TheGuardian.com. June 2, 2015

Topic 12

Excerpt From Report of the United Nations Water Conference, Mar del Plata, March 1977. United Nations publication, Sales No. E.77. II.A.12). © 1977 United Nations. Reprinted with the permission of the United Nations.; Excerpt From "Male' Declaration on the Human Dimension of Global Climate Change".; Quote from: "The Right to Adequate Food–United Nations High Commissioner for Human Rights"; Excerpt From 2030 Agenda for Sustainable Development (Section on Empowerment, Equality, Inclusion). United Nations Human Rights, Office of the High Commissioner. Reprinted with permission.

Topic 13

Excerpt from Iron.: An Illustrated Weekly Journal for Iron and Steel Manufacturers, Metallurgists, Mine Proprietors, Engineers, Shipbuilders, Scientists, Capitalists. 1823; A petition by Eli Whitney to the US Congress requesting renewal of his cotton gin patent, 1812; Excerpt from Cotton in India, The Illustrated London News, January 21, 1854.

Topic 14

Excerpt From Proposal of Gustav von Struve to the Frankfurt Pre-Parliament, March 31, 1848. Translated into English by Pearson Editor.; Excerpt From "Blood and Iron," speech by Chancellor Otto von Bismarck, September 30, 1862. Translation Copyright © 2020 by Pearson K–12 Learning Services LLC.; Excerpt From On the Constitution of the North German Confederation," speech by Johann Jacoby, May 6, 1867. Translation Copyright © 2020 by Pearson K–12 Learning Services LLC.

Topic 15

Quote from The War of the Golden Stool, 1900, Governor Frederick Hodgson in Indigenous Conflict Management Strategies in West Africa: Beyond Right and Wrong, edited by Brandon D. Lundy, Jesse J. Benjamin, Joseph Kingsley Adjei. © 2015 by Lexington Books and imprint of The Rowman & Littlefield Publishing Group, Inc.; Quote from: The War of the Golden Stool, 1900, Queen Yaa Asantewaa. The Black Woman in History by John Henrik Clark, 1975.; Excerpt from The Invasion of Mexico: Proclamation of President Juarez, 1862.; Excerpt from: Rahimatulla M. Sayani, Presidential Address to the Twelfth Session of the Indian National Congress, 1896.

Topic 16

Emmeline Pankhurst speech, June 24, 1915.; Account of "Louvain Horrors" by R.H. Davis.

Published in New York Tribune, August 1914.; Excerpt from: The Enemy at His Pleasure: A Journey through the Jewish Pale of Settlement during World War I. Translated by Joachim Neugroschel. Translation Copyright © 2002 by Joachim Neugroschel. Reprinted by permission of Georges Borchardt, Inc., on behalf of the translator.; Excerpt from: Memoirs of the Maelstrom, by Joe Lunn.

Topic 17

Excerpt From An Appeal to the Men of New Zealand by Mary Ann Muller, 1860.; A Timeline of Women's Suffrage Granted by Countries.; Excerpt From Suffrage Fallacies by Mrs. A.J. George, 1916.; Excerpt From "A Long Road to Women's Suffrage in Saudi Arabia, by Elizabeth Dickinson, Foreign Policy, November 4, 2015". FP Copyright © 2015. Reprinted by permission.

Topic 18

Excerpt From Their Finest Hour by Allan A. Michie and Walter Graebner, 1941.; Excerpt from Interview with a member of the French resistance, David P. Boder, 1946. Paris, France.; Frances Slanger, Letter from an American Nurse, published in Stars and Stripes, October 1944.

Topic 19

Quote From "Evolution of Korean Anti-communist Films and Its Conditions, Jo Jun-hyeong, 2011". KOFA (Korean Film Archive); Stephen Hardy; Andrew Holman; Spin Digital Media

Topic 20

Excerpt from The Arusha Declaration by Juilius Nyerere, 1967.; Excerpt from African Market Women: Seven Life Stories from Ghana by Gracia Clark. Copyright © 2010 by Gracia Clark. Reprinted with permission of Indiana University Press.; Excerpt from Genocide in Nigeria: the Ogoni tragedy by Ken Saro-Wiwa, 1970.

Topic 21

Excerpt From Convention on the Rights of the Child.; Excerpt From Malala Yousafzai: 16th birthday speech at the United Nations, July 12, 2013.